LIVIN'
ON THE
EDGE

A Guide to Your
Abundance Seeds

LIVIN'
ON THE
EDGE

A GUIDE TO YOUR
ABUNDANCE SEEDS

Tinker McAdams

atmosphere press

© 2021 Tinker McAdams

Published by Atmosphere Press

Cover design by Matthew Fielder

No part of this book may be reproduced without permission from the author except in brief quotations and in reviews.

atmospherepress.com

Preface

When I started this journey forever ago, I knew I was a little different than most. My background into the unknown started at a very young age. Seeing and feeling things that others did not (or would not admit to). You know how it is, seeing things that others don't, hearing that little voice that others don't. If you don't relate to this, then I don't think that you would be reading this book.

There's a presence out there that can touch you like nothing else. Some call this vibration; others refer to it as energy, Angels, Divine Guidance, or Source. Doesn't matter what you call it, it's there! This presence can give you the highest high or the lowest low, it depends on how you listen. The trick is being able to harness into that highest high and go for the grandest ride of your life.

I'm taking you on this journey to help you know that there is a way to become a part of this energy inside you. You were born into it. There are connections to the Other Side that are all your own. You don't have to have someone else do it for you! I've been in touch with my Guys for a long time and you can be in touch with yours too!

There are times that we all feel restless, that life could be more fulfilling and richer. Not with money per se (which has always been one of the main energy problems), but to be able to enjoy each day to a better attunement. To have more of a meaning. Knowing what me and you have been through, there has to be more to it, right?

Life should be more than a daily drudge. What I have been aware of in my own personal life has not been normal by any means. I'll start at the beginning so you can get to know me a little. It may be a slightly boring to you at first but stick with me. Then we can dig into what you can relate with through your life and see how to make those situations better for yourself through the help that you personally have on the Other Side and in your own life!

Through this book you will experience what I've experienced firsthand and hopefully you can relate and use it to see into this Divine presence that will guide you in the right direction that is just for you. I'm saying this because everyone is different. We have our own ways of learning and interpreting. We all have some kind of special ability, but no two humans are the same.

I will also try to cover what I have learned in natural ways. Our Earth gives us a wide variety of healing options. There is so much you can benefit from knowing what can help you heal mentally and physically.

Word of warning! I'm not your normal everyday person. In this book, I will tell stories, cuss, rant, dig, romp, stomp, voice, and not pull any punches. I'm real. That's what I want you to experience. The real down to earth every day working of coping and making the best of what life has to offer through the help of your own Guys, the ones that are the wonderful presence that can help you with your endeavors. I'll try my best to put things in layman's terms so this little book can help you through whatever you need.

This is my story. The life lessons that have been given to me—and there are many! How you can, in your own time, learn to listen to the ones that are trying to help you, guide you, that little voice that beckons you to listen, feel that presence and make decisions that can turn your life around. Whether it's money, love, or health or just knowing who you truly are. You can be guided by those that can see and will always do their best to make the right decisions for you.

In the pages that follow, I will try to cover any and all things having to do with how you feel, the reason why and maybe touch a nerve or awaken a sense that may help you with your journey. Life is about being happy. It's hard to explain sometimes but there is this energy, unexplainable vibration that can be tapped into. It's being a part of the universe that you never realized was there for you. Just for you!

Have you ever had a moment when this feeling came over you and it was so strong that it made your hair feel like it was standing on end? A moment when you were so in tune with the world around you that there was a feeling on being invincible? That's it! That is something that you can experience every day of your life. To be able to wake up in the morning and have a feeling that you are so glad to be alive! Once you are in this realm of living, it does not matter about money or power. It is all about knowing that you are beyond the normal, you are a Being that does not have to do as others do because there is a protection around you that no matter what happens you are taken care of, protected from whatever may arise in your life. Believe me when I say this, it is the most gracious, loving, and wonderful feeling. To know that there are others in the non-physical that care so much about you they will step in and guide you to a life that is so worth living.

Hopefully, it can rouse you to the realization that doing good and being in touch with what is whispered in your ear or what you feel can and does advance you in this physical form you are in at this moment to a better way to understand and be one on one with the non-physical. I will try to write it as though you are sitting with me and we are talking face to face.

My Guys have a lot to say, and through this book you will get firsthand what is out there for you through them. They are the reason this is all happening. They want you to know that everything you could possibly have, or any questions there may be, they can help.

So, let's get going. Buckle up! Get ready to embark on a new adventure!

"Finding yourself" is not really how it works. You aren't a ten-dollar bill in last winter's coat pocket. You are also not lost. Your true self is right there, buried under cultural conditioning, other people's opinions, and inaccurate conclusions you drew as a kid that became your beliefs about who you are.

"Finding yourself" is actually returning to yourself and unlearning, an excavation, a remembering who you were before the world got its hands on you.

Emily McDowell

Chapter I
A Word from My Sponsors

While working on this book, my Guys have guided, poked, and prodded me all the way through it. They have kept me in tune with the deed at task and wanted throughout the book to give you as a reader their personal message.

From this point forward some of the words you see will be theirs. I will let you know when they have to say their piece. They have waited patiently on me to get to this point of writing this book and want you to be aware and awakened.

There will be times that I will intervene, but this is mostly their time to send the message that they want you to know. There will be all aspects of ways to get to know yourself and your Guys. So here we go.

First message from my Guys:
Greetings and hello from beyond the veil. We are here to voice and discuss with you, things that are of importance. First off let us say that you are truly loved. Our hopes are for you to understand that there is always someone that cares for you through all that life has given. Our mission from this side is to help and guide you along your path.

There is much turmoil on our wonderful Earth. It is your and well as our goal as a group to try and make sure that you who are in the physical world realize how important it is to wake up and work with everyone and everything as a whole. The point of these words on paper is to help you reach out and find your own Guys, as Tinker has told you. There are those that need your help in accomplishing all of this for the greater good.

We on this side are full of love and light and want all to be able to help you experience the energy that is there for you. We see the struggle that is taking place all around you and again want to emphasize that we are here.

Let us tell you what it is like on our side of the veil. We are here as beings of light. When you pass, your physical body is gone and all that remains is your glowing energy. Others that you have been with will be waiting to welcome you. There is no pain, no grief. It may seem like a wonderful dream. There are harmonious sounds and beautiful lights. All is in sequence. The vibration of the Divine seems to overwhelm you. The love that is there will take you by surprise and fill you with joy. We too have been in the physical form and now that we are on the Other Side, we know how life is in the physical and can relate and help you.

From our side we see the struggle that everyone is having—money, health, love—we see it. Tinker has been a great receiver and she has tried to be a guide for others all her life. The point here is we need more of you. We need those that want to feel happy and share this happiness with all that you meet. Happiness is a wonderful energy that can grow, and it can outweigh any bad or negative that is out in your space and time. With happiness brings love, money, and true joy. Once you start this journey in the physical you will see the picture that we are trying to paint. You can achieve anything that your heart desires and all that will make you happy if you just try.

Earth has been a home for so many to experience great joys. She is of her own energy and vibration and feels the same way that all of you feel. She breathes just the same as you. All of you are her family and she loves you with everything she has. She is your mother.

The creatures around you are all made of the same elements as you. They are there and exist for the same reason as you do: to be able to feel love and happiness and to do their part in achieving their goal. You as humans must realize that they also need your help more than ever. Without them you are not the whole vibration that you need to be.

Let's start off with the basic need that you may have. Some have an easier time in prayer than meditation. Let us explain the difference of prayer to that of meditating. Either way it is the connecting with the vibrational energy that will help you connect with those that are there for you.

To pray is to actively attempt to touch the heart of the Divine. If you choose to pray, please try to make sure that there are no bad motives, so you can show the Divine that you are worthy of his blessings. Have good thoughts, seek to have the Divine's will for you. Feel the presence and be sure that whatever you ask for is the best possible purpose and not something that is a selfish wish. Prayer is useless if it causes harm to another.

With meditation you become one with the Divine. It is filling yourself with the vibrations of the universe. You are as near to the Divine as you can attain. This is the point where we meet the Divine that is within you in the physical. You become a part of all that there is. The whole process of meditation is a way to become part of the Divine which is the universal wisdom and will put into action things that are not yet happening in the physical plane. With that being said let's get started on how you can begin your journey into a more vivid light. A beacon for those that cannot see for the darkness.

Close your eyes. Feel all that is around you, take a deep breath and *feel*. Listen, listen for the smallest sound you can possibly hear. Feel the inside of yourself. The breaths, heartbeat, the pulsing from within. This is you, the *I am*. The own uniqueness that is only you.

Practice this as much as you can. The more you connect, the more you will see. Things will become more vibrant and vivid. There will be realizations that you never imagined. Take your mind to places that bring you peace. In the quiet, go within and connect with the Divine.

We are here to help you every step of the way. If there are questions that you need answered, this is the time to ask. Listen to what is being put in front of you. If you feel the need to do this during your dream state, this will work for you also. Put your mind at rest and ask for answers.

Each of you being connected have your own special light from which you shine. The feeling of what life is to you belongs to only you. Even though we are one, there is also slight difference between all.

You must connect to what is special for you. These are your dreams of ambition that only you can make happen. To get there you must find your path that leads the way. Some need to push while others need to pull. The path is for you to take. In meditation try to become one with the living whole of creations, forget the personal and all else except the oneness with the entire universe.

There will be obstacles and yields along the way that are only there to help you understand what is best for you. The secret is to find your peace within. Notice the small things while at times take a view of the large. There is nothing more beautiful than a clover in bloom or majestic as a mountain top.

Pull away from the noise of the manmade and connect with the natural. Take five minutes to feel the wind brush your cheek, which is Earth's touch. Listen to the movements of each creature you come in contact with. The lovely songs of birds in the morning or the charismatic chirping of crickets at night.

This is the true path of your meditation: to be able to connect with all that you are related to. This and everything around you are your stardust family that you are all made from. We as guides are here to help with what you may need or want. When you are happy so are we, and so is the Divine.

It fills us with such joy and eagerness when we see and feel the positive vibration and energy you as in the physical create. There is nothing more pleasurable to your Creator than to feel connectedness from you.

Take time, when you can, to connect. We see that it is a busy place where you are, and we understand if you cannot reach out every day, but please try. It is for your benefit as well as all others around you. Everyone needs help in one way or the other. Take time to notice. You can be Angels on Earth. Even the creatures that are around you need your help. They are a mere small token of showing your love. They feel as you feel, wanting to be loved and appreciated. It will always be returned what you show for them.

The tall trees blowing in the wind need to know that you are there for them. They are part of the stardust family too. They feel and communicate within themselves on a very deep measure. They have the ability to send out positive energy and vibration across miles and miles of our Earth. Connect with them and see how quickly your wishes can come true. They are there also to help. Send a message to someone far away and they can deliver.

If you reach out to us, we will let you know that we are here. We are always here. We have been with you since your non-physical to physical transformation took place. We want to communicate with you. Just ask for a sign and we will give you one. But you must be alert to the signs we give. They may be subtle at first but with time it will become apparent that our existence is real. So real that you may wonder why you haven't realized we were there before.

Talk to us, tell us what you need from us. We are the miracle workers that you always wanted but never realized you had. Being connected with us can and will make your life joyous and worth every moment of every day. The beautiful peace of mind that you have been striving for. With this you will find that all kinds of abundance will shine through!

Abundance comes in all shapes and sizes. To be happy each and every day is worth every moment you have. If money is truly needed, we can help with that too, we just don't want the *ego* to move in where it shouldn't be. Your life and existence in the physical are worth more than that. Keep the thought in mind that when you ask for large amounts that seem to allude you. Think of things coming to you like the flow of water. If it isn't coming through easily then something isn't flowing. Think again as to what you truly want. Clear your mind and seek what you truly need. We are here, and we are listening.

There is a great coming that we want you to prepare for. A time that will test all of us. We all must band together and get ready. There is much energy that is not in the realm of being connected. It has been collecting for a very long time and it is growing every day.

We as a stardust family must come together and right what is wrong. We as a whole can overcome this negative by being at our most positive. Our vibrations and energy combined with you can out do all the bad that has been coming forth. To say it plainly it is time to for all to hear the call to arms. So many of you are ready and need to get to the point of your freedom to make a difference. It has always been "we" not "I" that penetrates the bad that happens. There are those that can't seem to grip the knowledge that positive energy is out there for them.

This is something that has been seen on our side for a long time. Earth is calling for your help. It is more than just climate and environment. It is a tumor that has been growing that we and you need to extract. You in the physical have so much power to the point that you can make anything happen for the good, but you must band together and make it happen. We are there for you. We will be behind you every step.

Realize how much this negative energy has been growing. There are those in the physical that want nothing more than to have it all for themselves. They relish in the ideas and think that it can be taken with them. They see nothing but what they think is for their own good and will not give a whisper's chance to help others. It's an evil negative vibration that needs to be made into something less vibrant.

Why is all this happening, you ask? The answer is this: because there are so many that put pleasure in front of service. It is more important to have all the finer things that to take time to help others. This is where you can make the difference. Become a part of good and positive energy. Shine your light as bright as you can. Show each and every being that you care. From the smallest creatures to the largest forests. They need you as much as you need them. You will find that the more you give, the more you get. If you can give time to help, you can expect to reap. It is all part of the balance. Be the one that can say you did your part. Others will notice and want to do theirs.

Time for me to intervene:

What my Guys are trying to say is if we can put the hectic and stress on a back burner for a few moments each day and take the time to connect with our own positive energy, this will make the difference that can push back the negative. This is how we make the difference. Our positive vibrant physical selves can start to put a hole in the negative that is trying to overwhelm everything around us.

The more we do this the more there will be better results in the way we live and the outcome that is staring us right in the face. Times are hard, as we all know. People are struggling—including myself—with just the everyday things that go on day to day.

The subtle and gentle calming of the mind for long enough to connect with our own higher selves and those that are trying to help us will start to have a chain reaction. We can make a difference in the way things are.

Now back to my Guys.

Yes, Tinker is right. We in the non-physical—each and every one of us—try to connect with you. Our whole purpose is to make you the beautiful energy that you were meant to be. By connecting with us, you will start the rolling forward of better things. With things being better for all of you will in turn start to push back the negative that is trying its best to overwhelm.

We in the non-physical do not want to scare you or try to manipulate. You were put on Earth with free will. It is all up to you to try or not to try. We are simply saying that we can make a difference. With each and all of you there is a reason you are there. Every one of you are meant to be, even those that are walk-ins. You may not have been born physical, but you are a volunteer to help with all that needs to be done. We love you. We love all of you. We feel, with all that is happening on Earth, you are missing what is so important for you.

Start each day as if it is a fresh new life, because it is! It is a time to smile and be happy, always be happy! This is one of the great secrets. Happiness can and will bring you everything. If your heart desires, then be happy and ask for our help and we will do our best to see that it will happen.

Be kind to others. Kindness is another secret that helps in so many ways. Kindness shows that you are worthy. Worthy to receive what you have shown others. It is the most desired secret there is. When you are kind, the Divine smiles. It is a universal feeling of emotion both in the physical and non-physical. Kindness can release you and make you free to do what you need to do. When we see kindness on our side it starts a ripple that grows larger and larger. So, at any given time please show kindness.

There will be times when others around you will try to take advantage of your kindness. When this happens, just let them go and move on. There will be those that are very thankful for you being there for them. These are the ones that you want to be around because they will in turn be kind to others. Make this ripple the largest that it can be.

With these moments and perseverance, you will notice there is something happening that no one thought possible. There will be a great change in you and others around you. Just the thought of having more seems to happen with a quickening—as though it was a snap of a finger. Your life will have more in it than you could ever imagine.

Those that are not awakened will see a different person that is shining like a bright star. Everything that you wish for will be there. They will say amongst themselves, "Why is this happening for them and not me?" You will look at them with a smile on your face knowing that you have that connection with the Divine and your higher being. Nothing is impossible. This is the time to invite them and coach them if they let you. Show them that you are there to help them accomplish what you have. In doing this you will become brighter and more in touch with that around you. Life will become the most invigorating and happiness will never end for you.

Remember that we in the non-physical are rooting for you. That's our purpose and we share in your joy. Let's make these the best moments for all involved. Start each day knowing that you make a difference for all around you, be it human or creature. Work and strive to see the difference.

We hope that those who read these pages will forever be touched. Touched by ideas of being whole with abundance, prosperity, love, and great joy in living for your purpose. Be who you are! Don't let anyone or anything stop you from being the magnificent physical being that is there to make a difference. Stand strong and see the world as it should be. If you fall, get back up. Strive to see the world around you as a whole. We have heard the saying in your physical: *"Be all that you can be!"*

We hope that as time goes by and moments are counted, more will come of this and having Tinker sharing our thoughts with you. It is our greatest wish that the ones that guide you can come to light in your life and be able to shift and be with you to your full potential. It would be our greatest pleasure to be able to have all the non-physical and physical join and be as one.

May this book be a guide to that point and time. We look forward to seeing the change come forth. Remember we are always here smiling and putting forth our energy to help you.

Time to intervene:

In the following pages there are a lot of ways for you to be able to become the awakened soul you were meant to be. Throughout you can see the different aspects and most of what it takes to become aware and know that better times are coming. My Guys will put in their two cents when they feel the need to. I have become very accustomed to their making themselves known and these pages have come forth because of them.

We have worked together since I was small, and they have guided me to all the knowledge that is in this book and more. It can be a long journey to get to the point that you will realize you don't look at things the same way. So, be patient and take your time to digest everything.

Back to my Guys.

Many of you know what it is like to be ridiculed and abused. It is one of our greatest wishes that when this is seen by others both adults and children they would step up and help stop this. We see so many young ones taking their lives because of this treatment. This is the time to help because these souls could do so much for the better as adults. If only one child would stand by the one that is being abused, others would join suit.

You cannot blame the bullying of other children. They themselves have reasons for what they do. Each of you need to be the guiding light that can start the ripple of goodness to come through.

All of you together can and will make a difference. Be that light, show that you care. Pass on your knowledge and tell your children that they can make the difference in so many lives. Help them see goodness in all. They have their own guiding spirits that can help them too.

If we in the physical and non-physical work together and feel the goodness that can take place, it's only natural that there will be a goodness that will come forth and help with all. We see that there is a different vibrational energy, but the secret to getting to the point where things will get better is to go within yourself and feel that consciousness that resonates within. Believe us when we tell you it is there just waiting to be tapped into.

Try to be the person that shows their gratitude. Tinker likes to call this: Gratitude with Attitude! It is always nice to say thank you, but when you say it with a smile and actually make eye contact with others, it is noticed! She likes to throw in a few kind words to top it off and she knows when she leaves their presence, they remember her. The people that work in the stores that are visited on a regular basis seem to like when she walks in. They are treated with kindness and respect.

When you are picking a way to react with others keep in mind to try to be nice. It has a wonderful effect on all involved. Try to make sure you put a smile on someone's face.

*The soul is the same in all
living creatures,
although the body of each
is different.*

Hippocrates

Chapter II
In the Beginning

Since the beginning of man, we have looked for that answer of true happiness. Searching throughout every nook and cranny to luck up on bliss. Everyone—and I mean everyone—has that spark to find what will make them gleam. There have been all kinds of leaders to help us find our meaning, from gurus and prophets to conquerors of countries.

From the help of my Guys, my quest is to help you in finding your true self. I'm not any of the ones mentioned above, just one that has been aware of what is around and available to us since I was able to maneuver on my own. (You know: taking your first baby steps, speaking your first words).

I've always been a little different than others. Never was much of a follower. Never could understand why people would take the word of someone or something they say without making a quest on finding the awareness of true meaning for themselves.

Growing up in the Bible Belt where the actual buckle comes across to secure, it's been a real test to find my own way in a spiritual world. I had to learn at an early age to keep my mouth shut on what was happening with being in touch with the non-physical in my life as far as the guidance from others that were not in physical form. Sometimes I would slip and say something that would draw attention and at the very least get that side glare from someone, and I could tell they were thinking that I was probably mental, and they would keep their distance.

But I finally made it to adulthood when the spiritual age was starting to bloom. (Thank you! Geez Louise, I thought you'd never get here!) To have the experience of knowing there were others that were experiencing the same guidance. It can get mighty lonely not to have those that see the things and feel the energy that helps us maneuver through life.

Through all of this I have found that each of us have our own special gifts that help us make it. There are those that see auras. This always amazed me. To be able to see the colors that surround other people that make them unique in their own way. Each color tells them a type of personality that is linked to the color. Talking to those that can see those beautiful prisms of light, they had the same problem as me. At first you think that everyone can see this, but you find out quickly: Um, no! They *don't* see the colors. What you hear from them is, "What the hell is wrong with you?" and "Can I see if I can get you help with this problem?" (in other words, your brain isn't wired quite right, and you desperately need some kind of therapy!) or "HAHAHA what color am I now, if I fart will it change?"

With those that realize they have this capacity, in their heads they must think, "Hey, dude! It's not a problem, it's a gift to help me see that you're a true butthead!" But I'm sure just like the rest of us that see differently, they probably smile and make up some off-the-wall excuse to suffice.

Once you get on board with the gift or gifts that you have—yeah, you can have more than one—remember there will always be those that question you and your ability.

People are quick to judge! If you don't follow the status quo, then they will try their best to make life as difficult as possible for you. Just overlook this very narrow way of seeing things. You know in your heart and soul how you feel. No one can take that away from you. Hopefully one day they can forgive themselves. If not, you learned a lesson on how not to treat others. Be kind! Be understanding! If nothing else, just be there!

Oh, in case you haven't realized it, one of my gifts is that I see dead people. My personal ones are pretty much are with me throughout the day and the voices I hear. Yes, I have seen them. Many times, they have come to me in my dreams. One has appeared to have grown up at the same pace as me. Started out seeing him when I was young. He was a boy my age and has aged with me through the years. He appears to be a Native American male. There is another who is a very ancient old soul. He's also Native American. They both have always been there. The younger one has a sense of humor, the elder not so much. Both have seen me through thick and thin. They have protected me from so much potential turmoil.

For instance, just the other day while driving to work my Guys—this is how I always refer to them—just gave the warning "beware ahead" immediately I let off the gas and as soon as I rounded a blind curve there was a truck broke down with his flashers on half way in the road. Seems he had gone for help because no one was around the truck. But if I had not listened to the warning from them, I could have plowed into the back end of the vehicle. Seems they're always doing this to keep me on the safe side. I thanked them profusely for this one!

I see others too. This is one of my other gifts that I was

given. Well, sometimes it's considered a gift, and sometimes they can scare the hell out of me! Not the *Boo* kind of scare but the walk around a corner and there they are! I talk to them just like I talk to everyone else. When rounding the corner and seeing a person standing there in your own house when you thought you were alone, it takes about a split second to register physical or non-physical. My usual reply after nearly having a coronary is, "Stop that shit! Dammit to hell, what is it?" Then, I calm down and ask how I can help them.

So, let me tell you a little more about myself and where it all started. I seem to remember as far back as being a baby in my crib. There was one time I woke up with a small dog sharing my space with me! Maybe this was the beginning of the relationship I have with other creatures.

The first realization of the presence of others was when I had to be between two and three years old. We lived on a country farm with a backyard that seemed to go on forever. Located in this big backyard was a large tree with a massive tire swing. (Well seemed massive to me, I was around two!)

One day when I was playing on the swing, my mom stepped into the house to pour herself another cup of coffee. The kitchen had this beautiful large window made up of many different panes of glass looking out. It took up almost the whole wall. I'm sure as she was pouring her coffee, she glanced out to watch me play on the swing. In that short amount of time of her pouring and glancing, I was gone! Being a two-year-old there were no real rules that my little mind seemed fit to follow so I decided to adventure up the hill into the woods.

There I went, loving the birds singing and wind

blowing through the trees. I was just loving being in nature. Our little dog we had named Blackie was following me along the way through the little trail that blazed us up the hill farther and farther from the house. Finally, I sat down on a small log to look around and that was when I realized there was someone whispering in my ear to follow Blackie.

I stood up and Blackie immediately started guiding me back down the hill. He would run back and forth, nudging me down the trail we had followed. To me it was a wonderful play time. Just me and Blackie having an excursion all our own.

Once I got to the edge of the woods, I could see that there were all these people in our yard. Mom was crying. Blackie kept running back and forth helping me make it all the way down the hill to home.

Turns out I had been gone long enough that there was a search party of neighbors that had gathered to look for me. All I know is I was having a grand time until that little voice took advantage of my sitting still for a moment to get me back home through Blackie. That sweet little dog led me all the way back to Mom's feet. You could see the relief go through her as she hugged me tightly and neighbors were smiling and shaking hands. I can't remember if I got into trouble for taking off, but I do know that Blackie was a big hero for quite some time!

Animals seem to be more in touch with the wonderful energy that is available to all. They prove themselves time and again that they hear the calling. What Blackie did was just a small gesture of what they are capable of doing with guidance.

At the age of three years, that very important person

in my life who loved me unconditionally took a turn for the worse. My mom was getting us ready to go out to do our Christmas shopping. She had just put my coat on me while Dad went out to start and warm up the car. The house we lived in had a Dutch door that led into the kitchen. Mom had asked me to wait for her, and she turned to close the bottom half of the Dutch door with me on one side and her on the other. In a split second she let out a loud excruciating scream and fell to the floor. My dad came running in, saw her lying there, and picked her up to place her in a chair.

At that moment there was this empty feeling inside of me and that little voice telling me that Mom was leaving. I didn't cry, just couldn't get that feeling out. I don't remember much more about that day, just as the evening came, she wasn't there. It was just me and Dad, and I could tell he was lost.

From that moment to about two years in the future, I watched Mom go in and out of the hospital. There were times that she was home in a hospital bed. There was a lady there that would help take care of her. I remember Mom having her push the bed she laid on into the open front door so she could watch me play.

Cancer took her away. She died two weeks before my fifth birthday. Remembering my birthday party, there was a moment when for the first time I cried, really cried. I wanted my mom. I missed her!

Later, I had found out that she had breast cancer before I was born. Doctors had advised her and my dad if she could make it seven years after radiation treatment, she would be considered a survivor. The incident at the Dutch door happened six and a half years after treatment.

That horrible disease went from breast cancer to bone. The simple turn to shut the Dutch door had caused her leg to snap, and the bone broke into two pieces. There were nights when she was at home, I could hear her beg Dad to please kill her because she was in so much pain. He would reply that he could never do such a thing. This whole time they thought I was sleeping, but I heard everything. Every moment of her having to slowly give in to this horrible disease. She suffered so much. But when I was around, she was always smiling at me and showing me how much she loved me.

The whole time this was taking place, after being tucked into bed, I would see entities in my room just watching out for me. They were lying next to me or being beside me. It was like they were babysitting, comforting me while the whole time I was learning about death at a very young age. They didn't speak much, just made sure there was a comfort in my life.

For years I heard all about her and what a wonderful giving person she could be. She had always been the love of Dad's life. They had known each other since they were children. Went all through school together. Secretly, they and ran off one night—he was twenty and she the tender age of seventeen—and eloped. Kept the secret of their marriage from both sets of parents for over a year.

This kind of commitment played a very important part in how I grew up. Dad never remarried. He raised me as a single parent. This was during the early 1960s, so this kind of thing almost never happened and was unheard of for that time in history.

At the time of her death, we lived in Fayetteville, Arkansas, after moving from Albuquerque, New Mexico.

The doctors had advised that a more humid climate might help her recover from all the treatment of the cancer and radiation, so they had packed up everything they had and moved from New Mexico to a place that would make it easier for her to continue healing.

When all this was taking place, between the move to another state and her getting sick, there were many times that I spent with my grandparents. My grandmother would talk a lot about Angels, and I would listen intently. She let me know that they are always watching out for us. They would always be there whenever we needed them. Through these talks of Angels, I knew the voices had an identity! My Angels were watching out for me. Every now and then they would speak to me, letting me know I would be okay.

Once Dad finally pulled himself together, my life was filled staying with other people while he worked. I can remember two that had a direct impact.

The first one was a lady that had children of her own, a boy and a girl. She liked to bake us cookies and let us play a lot. Every day she would let us go get the mail for her. We had to walk down a hill and cross a road to get to the mailbox. One day as we were crossing the road to get back up the hill, a car came flying around the curve and was right on top of us before we knew it. The car swerved to the right to miss us, heading in the same direction as us (that was kind of DUH), but seems it was heading right towards me! I remember being moved to one side as my right hand reached behind me and touched the grill of the car. It came to a complete stop with the front end in the ditch. I crawled out from the ditch, but nothing was broken, just bad scrapes and bruises. The woman driving the car was screaming, "I hit one of those children, I hit one of those children!"

In my young mind I was thinking, "Yeah, lady that would be me!"

A crowd surrounded us, and an ambulance pulled up. About this time there was my Dad. He followed us to the hospital, where I can remember them washing out the wounds and bandaging me up. My left ankle got the worse of it. I still carry a scar to the top left of my ankle to this day. Seems a rock made its way in.

My dad made it a point to visit the lady one more time. I think he wanted her to see my banged-up condition. I remember him telling her that she need not send children to fetch her mail for her anymore!

There was another couple that had been friends with Mom and Dad that looked after me. They had two children of their own. From memory, I believe the man of the family worked with Dad. From that point on, they were the ones I would stay with until I started school. She didn't bake cookies but would come outside to play with us. They lived on top of a long hill. I could watch and see when my Dad was coming to pick me up. I would hear my little voices telling me that he was on his way and I would be watching.

There was a friend of my dad's that came to visit often by the name of Dr. Lemon. He was always laughing, and I'm sure he kept Dad's spirits up. They would always sit at the kitchen table at the end of the day and sip whiskey together. I think Doc Lemon helped my dad so much with getting closure over my mom. He always picked at me and made me feel warm inside. Great guy to have around to help with our little family.

One day I wasn't feeling very good, and my Dad had called Dr. Lemon to come by and see what may be wrong with me. As the day wore on, the worse I felt. By that evening when Doc got there, I was *sick*!

He diagnosed me with German measles and chicken pox at the same time. I had them both! He advised Dad above all else to keep me in a dark room for he feared that my eyesight could be severely damaged.

With this advice my dad went on a quest to find a place for me in our home. There was a coat closet that was just big enough for a cot to fit in. Dad cleaned it out and kept me in this completely dark closet. I remember being so sick! Once again, comfort from those that can't be seen were there. This time one of them was Mom. She cuddled me and helped me through my misery. Seemed like it was forever before I finally got over this. It was nice to feel Mom's touch again, the coolness of her hands making me better.

You as the reader will need to remember, this is my recollection from the age of two to five. I haven't even started school yet. It seems there was quite a bit of turmoil happening for a little person, but to myself it was a training ground for what was to come in the long term.

There is a fine line between the positive and negative. Balance is the key. Anyone can make good out of bad especially when they know there are others rooting for them, physical or not.

Through all my research and studying of those on the Other Side, we are born with two guardian Angels or energies (whatever you want to call them), that are there to look out for us. Our problem is our physical selves need to listen.

There have been times when I have felt like my two Guys have had to literally scream at me to get me to at least turn an ear their way. It seemed much easier when I was small. That's when your mind is open to all possibilities, not burdened with true troubles in life that comes from every direction when you are older. So, please sit back and gently turn the pages as you read and keep in mind this is just the beginning.

Most just want recognition that they can be seen. So many have passed without having closure from the physical side. I talk to them and let them know it's okay. I've had a few that have messages for the ones still here. Usually, it is someone I know. A few times I've had places where a loved one comes through and wants me to relay a message to a person I just met. This can be a hard thing to present to someone if they don't believe in the hereinafter like I do. But eventually I get the message to them. Hopefully they can take it with a grain of salt and accept what is being given.

There was one time that a friend and I were going to see a psychic that was having an event locally. It was around the holidays. Christmas had just passed and we were waiting for the new year to start.

My friend—we'll call her J—had lost a son years ago. He was murdered on the streets of Memphis just for what was in his pockets. She never had closure from this act of violence. The psychic was randomly selecting people in the crowd with messages that were coming through from passed loved ones. Needless to say, J was not one of them.

As we were leaving, I could tell that she was extremely pissed about the situation. She wanted so badly to receive a message from her son. For days after that we talked on the phone and she still was highly upset that nothing once again had been rendered about her son.

Then it happened. I was sitting on my couch and the way it was positioned in my living room I could see straight down my hallway. I looked up and realized there was a presence at the end of the hall. Leaned with his back against the left wall was a tall, blond, well-built young man looking in my direction. He seemed to hold back a little as though he was kind of shy and just watched me as I sat there. On and off I saw him in the same spot just like he was waiting for something. This went on for a couple of days before I finally asked him was there anything that I could do for him.

All at once this overwhelming feeling of love and compassion went through me like a bolt of lightning. Then it hit me! This was J's son C. He had come to settle what was going on with his mom. Seems he was a very polite and wanted my permission before he gave me any information. I could hear everything clearly of his thoughts and feelings. This went on for a few minutes and I knew that I had to call J and let her know what had happened.

She knew a little about what I was capable of, but we never got into detail. I let this sit with me for a day or two rolling over in my mind how to tell her. My Guys were nudging me to give her a call, but I was reluctant because I didn't know exactly how she was going to handle this. Finally, the time came.

On a Sunday morning after having my coffee my Guys were relentless. All I could hear was "DO IT NOW" over and over—they were not giving me any peace at all! Okay, Geez! Let me take a few breaths and I'll do it.

Taking a deep breath and hands shaking, I called J and talked for a moment. Then softly I let her know that there was something I needed to discuss with her. My first sentence was "Are you sitting down?'

She knew when I said that, that it was serious. Her reply was, "I am now."

As I took a deep breath, that feeling I had when C appeared came rushing back. All I could think to myself was "Just maintain, just maintain."

"J, your son came to see me, and I have a message for you." (All the time I'm fighting back these tears from the feeling of all this love and compassion. These weren't tears of sorrow but of joy and happiness).

"Okay," she said.

"Okay, here we go. C came to me the other day and wanted me to let you know that he is fine. There is no pain of having to leave except your heartache that he can feel! He's sorry for how he left you behind, but he loves you so much and to please stop worrying about him. He knows that you love him dearly and that you are not to blame. It just happened. He didn't linger here for long after the gunshot. Please stop worrying about him."

At that point I was bawling like a baby. J was bawling like a baby. We were both just sitting there on the phone wailing. (Where are the damn tissues when you need them?)

Finally, J spoke up and let me know that this was the anniversary of the day he was killed. She gave me the whole story of what had happened. Her son had come to visit her for Christmas and had decided before he left to go to Memphis and do some shopping and visiting.

He was met on the street by someone that demanded

money from him. He handed his wallet over willingly, and then the guy shot him at point blank range. It was a needless death. J was a retired registered nurse. She had always felt that if she had been there maybe she could have saved her son. She blamed herself because he had come to visit her. All these years she felt in some way that he may have blamed her in that last moment of his life.

At that point I let her know of the feelings I had once he and I were communicating. There has never been a time when I felt so much love for another person. My conclusion from it was that J and her son had a very close bonded love for one another. J had several children, so C wasn't an only child. Everyone should wish to be this close to the children they raise. I commend her!

From what I understand from my Guys, once you pass you just move from one dimension to another. You are aware of this beautiful energy and the colors! Everything is so vivid. There are those waiting for you to come through and greet you with such never-ending joy.

Once someone moves to the non-physical there is a realization that things need to be done on that side too. We don't need to mourn for a long period of time—they're still there when we need them—but never letting go and moving on from their death holds them back from what they need to do. Life is constant on both sides.

Message from my Guys

When one passes over, everyone is here to greet them. We see a lot of the problem as when those that pass in a violent way are at first dazed and confused. There was no lingering and getting ready to pass. You may "feel" them around you because they are! They cannot understand why this has happened. There are also those that wish to have closure on the physical before they go about what needs to be done in the non-physical. It is their way of having their final goodbye.

If one of your loved ones comes to you, explain to them why they are there. You don't have to actually talk (though you can if you want), but in your thoughts let them feel the love and warmth that you have always had for them. Be calm and let them know they are always loved and will be remembered. At first passing, they will come in and out to you looking for reassurance that everything is fine. Now is the time for you to be kind and loving.

Please be patient with them and let them know you love them and wish for them to be at peace. As for you in the physical, please help as much as you can. Let them move to their new dimension with much love. Just as being in the physical, once you return to the non-physical there is a place for you to go to and start your journey there. We will be here for them to make sure everything is as it should be.

Be aware that your loved ones will never be alone. The hurt and pain remains in the physical world. On this side of the veil there is nothing but joy and happiness in all the energy around us. Rejoicing is abundant! Everything is a celebration, and all falls into place as it should be. Once they have settled, take our word that they are watching out for you and want only the best. The true love that was felt there on Earth remains and lives here also. Don't be surprised if every now and then you can feel their presence with you. When Tinker is visited, she explains it to be a very wonderful warm vibration of the best kind.

Always let them know that you love them to visit, give

them a smile and be happy! It is a time for rejoicing and realizing that life is eternal. It is not a passing away but a passing over. You can still laugh and joke with them. Having a visit from those you love should and will warm your heart!

*We are not what we do,
what we say,
or even what we think.
Our essence is something
beyond all this.*

Headspace (app)

Chapter III
We Move On

Now back to learning a little more about me and how life's schooling prepared me for more of what could be expected in the future.

The time had come for me to start school. Oh fun, fun. No, I'm kidding. I absolutely hated it! Getting up early every morning, getting ready, and then having to ride the bus. Nope, not having it.

Once I settled into first grade, the teacher decided that I could not and would not be left-handed. She would literally tape the pencil in my right hand to make me use it.

That's when I decided that I was not going to school. I threw a huge fit every morning, refusing to get ready. Finally, after arguing and getting my butt busted, Dad asked me why I didn't want to go. Told him about the pencil ordeal, and he blew a gasket!

He loaded me in the car, headed straight to the school, and proceeded to chew on whomever got in his way. My Dad was not a man that you wanted to cross if his temper was coming through, and it was on full steam.

All that being said, I no longer had a pencil taped to my right hand! Still didn't like school but had won one battle.

Shortly after that, we moved from this place and my life changed again. Dad's work transferred him to another state to open up an office for the company he worked for. Here we come Tennessee!

This was back in the early 60s, as I've said before, and

his moving was something he had to do on his own. I had to stay with my aunt and uncle for about a month or so until he got us all settled in. With all the moving, my schooling kind of took a back seat.

To look back, it seems that my dad just couldn't bear to live in the same house where Mom died. He needed a new start in different surroundings. He found this small town in the middle of Tennessee to raise me. One of those towns where everyone knows everyone.

Once he got me all moved in, the house was much smaller than the one before, and it was in town. No longer was there the big back yard and tire swing. Time to learn to live close to others, I guess. The good side of it was that next door there was a girl my age with a bunch of brothers. We hit it off right away, so now I had a friend.

I started back to school. This time it seemed different. My teacher was a stern but very kind person. She worked with me after school to help me catch up on all that I had missed. A gentle soul, but she wouldn't put up with much nonsense, and believe me it seemed that the young boys in a small Southern town could sure dole out nonsense. All the while I watched and observed. Why should they have all the fun!

That's when I realized that I was slowly turning into a full-fledged tomboy. At the time, I was taller than the other kids (boys included), long legged and ready to get into anything that wanted to dare me. That seemed to happen on a regular basis. Why is it children always must test to see how far they can go. There was always a smart word and then time to tumble. My poor Angels were there with their soothing voices, but sometimes I just didn't want to listen.

Life was a lot different with just me and my dad. He was a headstrong, determined kind of guy. One thing that I noticed from the beginning was he talked to me like I was more than just a daughter. The older I got, the more he confided in me.

He always believed that women were just as capable of doing things as men. He had a lot of sayings that I still live by and have distilled in my own three sons. He never let me quit anything. If I started it, I had to finish it. One of the sayings was, "You can do anything you set your mind to." Years later I realized he was one of us, someone that believed in the power of ever-giving energy. Those that know there is that higher power and if you work with it, it will work for you!

Sometimes I thought that man had the Midas touch! Anytime he needed something in his life, it seemed it wasn't long until it happened. If you ask, you will receive! I was raised with the Law of Attraction. But I was taught to be humble. No one should be above anyone else. Be there for those that need you. Once you have helped, move on to the next person or creature that may look like they are in a place that you can help.

One thing that needs to be realized: abundance is not just money. It's all and everything the universe can give. If you are happy and love each day that is given, you are rich. Richer that most that are around you.

Learn to defeat the negative that sucks the life out of you. It's a blessing to leave it behind. Don't let it eat at you. You must pull yourself up each day and be determined that it's going to be better than the day before. Think of yourself as flowing water. Those that are in touch with their ability realize this and often tell others the same that

I'm telling you.

Most of the time you just drift along, and everything is the way it should be. When times of turbulence come in, just flow with it knowing that before long, you will be drifting again. But remember if you try to reverse your course and move in a way that doesn't feel natural, you are trying to move upstream it will be a fight for you every inch of the way. That is the way life is. There will always be something that may cause turbulence and it's up to you to realize that you need to find a different path.

Say, for instance, you have a decision to make on something that has come up in your life. Ask your Guys and the universe to help you. If the wrong move is made and it begins to be a struggle, know that you're trying to move upstream. Give up that fight and start moving in the other direction. See what you can do to smooth out the water. If you give them a chance, they will give you the answer you need to make things right and remember there are always others around you watching and wanting to help.

There was another saying my Dad had: "*Can't* could never do a damn thing!" He never allowed me to say, "I can't!" and then just let me go about my business. His answer was always with the question, "Why can't you?" You always must try at whatever it is you need done in your life. Be determined to achieve whatever is thrown at you. It can be done, never forget that! But remember the flow. Ease your mind and go with it. Feel that wonderful energy pump back into you and breath it all the way in.

Here is a little exercise that I learned to do in my teen years. It helps you to relax and work with the universe. It's kind of fun too!

You may have heard of it: evaporating clouds. Yeah, that's right, making clouds disappear. If you have never tried, now's the time. All you need is a sunny day and some fluffy clouds passing by. It does require you to be outside in the fresh air (sorry, it's a requirement). Start out with a small cloud and work your way up.

First, just relax and sit your butt down on the ground. Look up in the sky and enjoy the view for a moment. As you're sitting there, find a nice little cloud that seems to be just waiting for you! Now start to stare at the cloud as if you know it like a friend you haven't seen in a long time. Feel that nice warm feeling of being with that great little friend. Relax your mind and start seeing the little cloud slowly getting smaller and smaller. Don't worry, you're not hurting the cloud—it's just air and water! Before you realize it, the cloud is gone.

What you have done is harnessed energy into an object. We and everything around us is energy. Some faster, some slower. Even rocks have energy. The beings that visit you in non-physical form are now pure energy. Imagine the possibilities when you have learned to work with that energy. There's a word for it: manifestation. Oh, how I love this word!

Manifestation is a wonderful way to move along on your journey in life. It takes a lot of stress out of having to live in a fast paced ever changing world we now live in. But, there's a catch. There's always a catch. You can't just wish it and it will happen. You must work at it. You see there is a natural law. It's all a flow, just like water. If you try to push, you'll go against the flow.

Here is another exercise you can do to learn how to manifest. The next time you're out driving around, say headed to the store or going shopping, start thinking about getting a nice parking spot that is close to the entrance so you can just jump out and go inside. Just think about it, no pushing, no wishing, just think, "You know, it would be nice to have a parking spot close to the door." Just imagine when you pull up, there it is, a spot reserved just for you! It works, and this is one of my favorite things to do! Oh, yeah, and always be grateful for being able to do this. Usually after I have parked, I throw out a "Thank you, Guys" because it always pays to be nice and realize things are working out for you.

Oh, and I can't forget this one! Bending time. Have you ever been running late for whatever life is dishing out for you at any given moment? Seems no matter how hard you try on that particular day, you're running late! Try this and see if it makes things a little better. If you are going full speed, just take a deep breath and tell the universe that you need to get there at this time, "Please work with me" and "I would be most grateful." When I do this, it seems that all the streetlights come out green, I'm going at a good steady pace when, low and behold, I make it with a couple of minutes to spare! You see, time is an illusion. It is an instrument developed by man. It can be manipulated. Don't forget at the end of your journey to always say thanks.

Like I said before, I'm just an average person moving along in this world trying to do the best for myself and others around me. We all must get along as best we can. Sometimes it's hard, I know that better than anyone. Just keep doing what is necessary to make life better than before.

Recently I was outside doing a little yard work and

looked down at my feet and there was a shingle from my roof! We had some bad weather with rain and strong winds, and it seems it took a toll on my poor old roof. After taking time to look up and investigate the damage, my first thought was, "Well hell, how in the world am I going to be able to afford a new one?"

I pondered on it for a while and knew there was no way I could come up with thousands of dollars to replace what needed to be done.

So, I turned it over to my Guys and the universe. My thought was, "Okay, Guys, just guide me in the right direction to get this done." After that I just let it go, keeping my mind open to a little voice or push that would get this problem done for me.

Came home from work one day, and it had probably been a few weeks since I had thought about the roof. Sat down to enjoy a cup of coffee and there was a knock on the door.

Two young gentlemen were standing there on my porch. I stepped outside to keep my dogs from barreling out the door and licking these poor two young men to death! They were going around the neighborhood with a company that does repairs on homes with damages. I thought to myself "Oh boy, here we go!" They had noticed my roof and wanted to see if I was interested in what they had to offer in getting it fixed. Being who I am I listened for a moment to what they had to say. Finally, I spoke up and let them know that I didn't have a lot of money, and I couldn't afford to have the roof replaced. We went over how much damaged had been done and they thought they could help me get it replaced through insurance. I would only have to pay the deductible. "Hmmm, you know," I thought, "I could probably swing that!"

They climbed up on the roof, went over the shingles, and marked all the damaged ones with an "x" in chalk. They asked who my insurance was through and proceeded to write up the necessary paperwork to get it done. All I had to do was make the phone call to my insurance and see if they would approve it. After they left, I immediately got online to check out the credentials of this company. Turns out they are highly recommended. So I made the call and now have a nice new roof. Didn't have to pay for anything until the job was done and I approved of the work. Now my roof is new and has a warranty. Once again: thanks, Guys!

You're probably thinking that with common sense I should have known that a phone call needed to be made to the insurance company, but I hate hassles and having to find someone to do the work. With this method of asking, it was laid out right in front of me!

Do you see what I'm getting at here? If you will work with the universe and the wonderful ones that have been assigned to help you with that natural way of just flowing, everything will work out. Learn to slow down, no matter what the world is throwing at you. If it seems that life is biting your ass, first tell it to let go and take a deep breath. Get that wide view in your head. Take a deep breath and start flowing. I'll say it again: *you can do anything you set your mind to!* Good or bad, so it might as well be for good.

Through the years of going on this quest, there is an awareness in our minds, and with just a little time and effort, it can develop into an ability that is both exciting and stimulating. The world will start to unfold. Once your awareness deepens, it seems that there are all these new dimensions. A world of all kinds of possibilities.

Think back into your own past and I bet you can recall a dream or a thought that seemed to foretell something that happened in the future. How many times have you thought of someone and within a day or two you get a call or text from them or you think of someone in the past and low and behold you run into them face to face.

There are times that I have talked to others that had a vision of someone being right next to them. They see their face as clear as day only to find out that the person they had seen had passed away. Seems the universe tries to let you know things that are happening to prepare you for what is to come.

For myself, they usually appear a few days after they pass to the Other Side. Their appearance seems to be when they were at an age of youth and vigor. You know, their best days while they were here. Full of energy and ready to take on the universe. Maybe that is just for a benefit to me. I don't really know the answer to that question, but I always recognize them for who they are.

Message from my Guys

The person that has passed reflects to when they were at their best. Energy on the Other Side is so much more vibrant. It is positive and makes the "youth" come out. This is the reason for the appearance. There is this vibration of everlasting. So, they reflect what is felt.

There is another force at hand that seems to walk with this: precognition and intuition. Knowing something that is going to happen before it does. This is another gift I have. There are so many things out there that can help you. We'll cover this more in later chapters.

*Your soul doesn't care
what you do for a living—and
when your life is over,
neither will you.
Your soul cares only
about what you are being
while you are doing
whatever you are doing.*

Neale Donald Walsch

Chapter IV
Living with the Other Side

When those that have passed finally realize where they are, I honestly think they seek out those like me. There have been so many entities in my home at any given time. Most are just passing through, but there are, like I said, those that want messages relayed to their loved ones here.

Besides having this ability to see, I'm also very empathetic, I mean *very* empathetic. Watching TV can be excruciating sometimes. When there is a scene where someone gets hurt, I feel it. If you ever meet one of my boys, just ask them. More on empathy later!

From what I understand from my Guys, once you pass you just move from one dimension to another. You are aware of this beautiful energy and the colors! Everything is so vivid. There are those waiting for you to come through and greet you with such never-ending joy.

There was a book I read that helped with this understanding. The name of it is *The Afterlife of Billy Fingers*. The author is his sister Annie Kagan. If you haven't read it, this book goes into detail on what to expect once you cross.

All of us will cross at one time or another. The feeling from my Guys is if we prepare now, it will be much easier once the time comes. We let too many physical material things overcome us on this Earth, and it interferes with the development of our spiritual awareness. The worldly things we possess mean nothing in the long run. The only thing that matters is how you as an individual prepare for this next stage of your life and to try to do the best you can while you're here. Helping others is a big jump in preparing.

Being in the non-physical is a learning experience just like being on this side. My Guys give me the feeling that our own personal entities are there for us and are preparing for their next own personal endeavor. They try so hard to help us in any way they can. The goal is to be the best you can be. Yes, it's nice to have great comforts here in our physical bodies, but did you help anyone along the way? Have you ever seen someone looking so downtrodden and stopped to see if there was anything you could do for them? I don't know how many times I have seen someone in the parking lot with a sign saying need money for gas or food. I always stop and give them a couple of bucks to help. It's not my job to judge others!

When at a restaurant and it is time to leave, I always make sure I leave a tip. Life here is a lesson, and what kind of lesson are you leaving for others if you don't do your part in helping? That waitress is probably a single mom busting her ass to be able to feed, clothe, and keep a roof over her children's heads. Pay it forward; it's the nicest and best thing anyone can do. It's nice to see people smile.

We are all sparks of our Creator. My goal is to make sure that my little spark is showing happiness and giving to others. The feeling I get is when I feel good about myself and what I have done, my Creator feels that too! Wouldn't you rather have your All Mighty receive beautiful vibrations and energies from you? Doing a little each day can make a difference.

What you are achieving is the moment. Moments are precious. These moments are more precious that all the money or jewels you could ever collect. To waste precious moments is to be cheating yourself out of a thing greater than any life you may live. Your soul is forever! Why not develop it to the best of your ability? To be able to progress to the ultimate life to live on the Other Side. Being your ultimate self not only helps you but helps your Guys too. Do you think that they want to try to help you and get nothing in return? They work through us on the physical plane to make themselves better for the ultimate life for which all our souls yearn. To be able to have that ultimate tranquility.

Life never stops. Always try to help others, whether they are physical or non-physical. The ultimate goal is perfection. To be able to say, "I did my best." When you leave here and travel to the Other Side, you have advanced as far as you can during this life span.

To give a perfect example, look at the life of Jesus Christ. Every day was a gift for him. Always trying to do what was best. Always trying to help others. From the beginning of living in a humble existence to striving to teach that you should give as much as possible.

He is proof that life is eternal. He rose again and life went on for him. It still goes on for him. Just because you leave here doesn't mean that you don't go on to another place in that moment. He moves on through infinity and he is proof that at last you can be pure and whole.

He had many gifts too. He even mentioned that everything he did we can do. It's there just waiting to be explored in your mind and to make it happen. All that is left is to take the initiative and see the possibilities that are available.

Another example is the Buddha. Here's a man born

into a life of wealth and privilege. Had the world at his feet. Destined to be a king in his country. But even with all that, he wasn't happy. Buddha knew there was something else to it. Life was more than all the material things.

He went out one day and saw how others lived. Sickness, poverty, and death. But amongst all of this he witnessed those that were happy without the things that go with it. His realization was that it doesn't matter how many worldly possessions we have, we all are going to end the same way. With much thought he finally decided to secretly leave and find out what true happiness was. He trekked for a while and finally one day sat down at a tree and made up his mind that he would go into meditation until the truth of life came to him and he could be a benefit to others. He realized that it is all about the here and now. This man was an inspiration to many and still is. His teaching is known around the world. He never lacked at helping others.

His dying words were, *"I can die happily. I have not kept a single teaching hidden in a closed hand. Everything that is useful for you, I have already given. Be your own guiding light."*

So, as you go about your business in everyday life, just think about taking that extra moment in time, be it energy or money to aid someone in trouble or being the jester to make someone laugh. Be a better person for your actions. This can be one of the most spiritual things you could ever do. Give others inspiration by example and prove that there are times when nothing is better than a helping hand. You can't change what you've done in the past, but you can make a better future. There still are those of us that care and want to help. We are becoming few and far between. Step up to the plate and be seen.

Here's another example, for instance. A few years back my oldest son was saving money for a trip he wanted to take to Ireland. Part of our family heritage is of Irish decent. He had been saving for a while, and then one day he got a phone call.

A friend of his that had just had a baby was at the hospital with the newborn. Apparently, the child was having seizers. The hospital refused to admit the baby without money up front. (You know the lack of being able to afford insurance speaks wonders.)

The young man had called my son to see if he knew of people that could help with the money that was needed to get the baby admitted. My son asked how much was needed to take care of this problem. It was a couple thousand dollars. He told the young man he would be there shortly and have the money for the baby. On his way he stopped by the bank and pulled out every dollar he had saved for his trip and gave it to this young family trying to save their child.

Knowing this made me one of the proudest Moms ever! To know he gave every cent he had to help was one of the kindest acts he could have done. After all this, they were able to help the child, and he returned home.

I don't think my son has started another savings account for that trip. He was just glad the money was there when it was needed. There is a reason for everything and his was served to the best possible manner.

Acting selflessly is the best way to further yourself. But, there are those that will take full advantage of you when you try to do what is best. I've said this before, and I'll say it again. Help those that need help and move on to the next person. Don't be taken in by those that dwell on the generosity of others. Seems in this day and time there are more and more of those that love to take advantage and feel no remorse for it. Best to step away from this kind of action. They will pull you deeper and deeper and once you can give no more, they disappear. Leave the leeches alone. To me they are mere blood suckers. My good nature is better for turning away from their never-ending whining and despair.

Now let's get into the best way to connect with your own personal Guys: the act of meditation. This is not an easy thing for me to do. My mind is constantly in action. Forever thinking and going, researching and diving into anything that sparks my interest. But, every now and then I go into my subconscious and it is the most beautiful endeavor I can take.

Most of my friends that I have grown up with have now traveled over to the non-physical. It's a wonderful thing to be able to visit with them. They have been the ones that have given me the firsthand accounts of what it is like to be there. Never have I heard a negative word out of any of them. They all have their own definition of what this heaven is all about. One thing is for sure, though, there is no more pain or grief. Nothing but pure happiness to finally see what ecstasy truly is. Let me give you an example.

I had a friend that I met when we moved here to Tennessee. We were both six years old and he was one of those boys that challenged me that I wrote about earlier. We grew up together not really being the best of friends but constantly saw each other on a regular basis.

We finally stirred up a friendship once we were older

and over our wild, youthful ways. He had his idea on life, and I had mine. Needless to say, we finally found some things we had in common and became the best of buds.

He was a Christian but didn't condemn me in what I knew to be my truth. We became like brother and sister, nit picking at each other at every turn. His nickname for me was Pony Class (because I had a Shetland pony when I was young and graduated to bigger horses as I got older), and mine for him was Horn Dog. (Yes, you can just imagine what he liked to talk about with that nickname). We were completely honest with each other and I loved some of our conversations.

One fine Sunday morning he called me. Here's a gist of the conversation.

"Hey, Horn Dog, what's up?"

"Oh, Pony Class, just a lazy Sunday here for me so I decided I would start reading the New Testament." (Hmmm, I thought, again!)

"Horn Dog, why are you reading the New Testament again? You always read the New Testament. Why not for once you read the Old Testament? There is a lot of things going on at that time. A great way to learn of our history. I loved reading it, gave me an insight of our beginnings. It was a time for mankind to serve at the best he could be and besides, looks like it would have been kind of cool to live to be 900 years old!"

His reply was, "Well, Pony Class, the Old Testament for me is nothing more than sex, drugs, and rock and roll! I seem to get more out of the teaching in the new part."

I laughed at his way of thinking! Only Horn Dog could put it in that perspective. We talked for a while as always, his plans for the coming week, where he was going, and who he was doing.

There were times my friend would become dark and inward with himself. As always, one of us would call the other. When this would happen with him being not quite himself, I would give him space. It would take him a couple of days to pull out of his funk, and then he would be the lighthearted great guy he always was.

He had been a registered nurse for quite a few years but had suffered multiple heart attacks, so finally he decided to step back from that occupation and endeavor on doing his own thing. He had made quite a bit of money for himself dealing in stocks and commodities. Always had the mind of making things happen.

One day he called, and I could tell that there was a different *feeling* going on. We talked for a moment, and then he hit me with it.

"Pony Class, I need to talk to you on a serious matter." (Deep breath here, I could feel what was coming).

"Okay, Horn Dog, I'm here, and you know I'll help in any way that I can."

He hesitated for just a moment, putting what he was thinking into how he was going to tell me. "Pony Class, I really don't need your help with anything. Just wanted to let you know that I'm throwing in the towel. I'm feeling its once again time for me to get another stint in my heart. But I'm not going to do it. I'm tired, and it's time for me to move on."

I sat there contemplating, not quite knowing what to say. I could feel this dread go through me. Here was my friend being open and honest. Realizing what he had just told me, I had to get a grip on myself and be the friend he expected me to be. So, I tried to stop my heart from racing, keep that feeling of total anxiety from taking over, and then just quietly let out another deep breath. After getting a grip on myself and putting my thoughts together, I had that dreadful question in my head that I needed to ask.

"Horn Dog, are you telling me that you are getting ready and preparing to pass over?"

I could tell it was hard for him, but I was so glad that it was me that he trusted. Out of everyone else in his life this important phone call was made to a very trusted friend.

"Yes," he said, "Pony Class, I know that you are the one person that understands what is going on with me. You have a different way of looking at all of this, and I just needed to have a sounding board on what I'm about to do."

My heart sank! To realize that I'm about to lose one of the best friends that I could ever have on this physical plane hurt. We talked extensively on what all was about to happen. He asked me several questions on what my outlook was on where and what he was about to partake in.

The one thing I strived to let him know was that he had to keep in touch with me when he moved over to the Other Side. At first his reply was, "Do you really believe that I can do that for you?"

"Sure, Horn Dog! Prove to me that what I know is true. Let me know firsthand what it's like. Keep me posted from time to time how things are going. We can still be friends and talk, just not as frequently. Let me feel your presence now and then."

We finally ended the conversation and the rest of the day left me in the deep thought that here is a man that all his life he made his own decisions on how his life should go. Now, he once again was taking control of his, even in death.

It wasn't long after that that Horn Dog left us. This is one of those times that I felt a great loss. There was someone that constantly picked at me, poked fun, and made life here much lighter and enjoyable. We had lots of laughs and at times deep conversations on every subject imaginable. He was someone that challenged my intelligence on every level.

From what I was told, he had been out one night, came home and was getting ready to turn in. It was late so he decided to make a phone call to ask a friend if they would give him a ride to the hospital. He knew this was it and knowing him he didn't want to die at home. He needed that closure knowing that everyone would know in a short amount of time that he was gone. He passed quickly. Within a few hours he had left from this world.

A few days later, the feeling came over me to try to meditate. After having my morning coffee, I settled in and told myself that this was the time for my friend to come through. In a matter of moments, I heard his voice. Horn Dog was there!

"Horn Dog, how are you? What's it like? Are you okay? Tell me all about it! Have you seen your Mom, Dad? What's up?"

He laughed at me! The person I saw in my mind was the guy I remember in high school. The long lanky dude with dark, wavy, shoulder-length hair. He had a big smile on his face that could light up a room.

"Slow down, Pony Class! I'm here and everything is great. It is more beautiful than you could ever imagine. Such peace and tranquility. I don't hurt anymore. Yes, I've seen all my relatives and they are glad to see me. I just wanted to let you know that you had the right idea on life here. I'll keep in touch with you, especially the next few days."

This gave me total peace. Knowing that my good friend was being his total great wonderful self. My heart felt lighter knowing this. It brought joyful tears for me. Thank you, Divine, for giving me such a wonderful friend.

After meditating for a while longer, I got up feeling very glad that my friend was okay. He is now able to see the whole not just a part. The next few weeks was full of him popping in and out.

One time as I was getting ready to take a shower he came through and made the comment, "Not bad looking for an old broad!" (Here's that split second of realizing physical or non-physical!)

"Horn Dog get out of the bathroom! Dammit, let me take a shower." He laughed and went on about his way.

Another time I was getting in my van and was looking around to where I might have put my cigarettes. There he was again, right behind my right shoulder.

"Pony Class, you don't need those damn things!" A little startled at first, but I immediately knew it was him.

"I know, Horn Dog, but it's my decision, not yours. Where are they?" After a few minutes I found them next to a place I would have never looked. "Horn Dog don't start hiding shit from me. It's not funny!"

Once again, he laughed and went on his merry way. He was getting way too much enjoyment out of pranking me!

He still pops in from time to time. Still that long lanky guy with shoulder-length hair. I miss our frequent talks on the phone, but just knowing that he is there for me now and then suffices what we once had and still have in a beautiful friendship.

Wouldn't you love to visit with someone that you love and care about that has passed from this world? You can! It is just setting your all-powerful mind into letting it happen and meditation is the way. Plus, keeping your mind open for the possibility. Everything takes time and practice. I knew early on that they were there, but I had no idea how to call on them whenever I felt like it. Keep practicing and asking them to pay you a visit before you start your meditation, or when you are turning in for the night and desire to have them visit in your dreams.

For myself, I get this feeling of needing to go into my subconscious, a drowsy feeling comes over me, kind of like they are making a call and I need to pick up. Pay attention to how you feel. They will let you know when they are there.

The best way I have found to get to the point of being in touch I learned from an app called Headspace. After getting relaxed sitting in a chair or actually lying down, find a point somewhere in the room to focus.

Slowly close your eyes and start at the top of your head with a feeling that there is this cleansing light. Have the light slowly move from the top of your head down all the way while focusing on relaxing as it moves downward.

Once it has reached your toes, start counting your breaths. Inhale is 1, exhale is 2, inhale 3, exhale 4. Keep this going to the number 10, then start over with number 1.

If your mind wanders, let it go for a moment and then start back with the counting. This keeps your mind focused on going inward.

Soon you should reach that point of being totally in your subconscious. You will know when you are there. It is one of the most peaceful feelings that you can get.

Remember, practice makes perfect. I myself have a hard time getting to this point, but once I'm there, oh, what a bliss it is!

Often, I will set an alarm to have myself come out of this. Once you reach it, you may find you want to stay!

Message from my Guys

We love when Tinker can come and visit. We in the non-physical try to make this the most inviting time. There is nothing more joyful than to be with our physical being on the Earth. This is the time for you to connect and feel what we feel. It not only uplifts you but us as well.

It is one of our most joyous occasions! It makes it easier to connect and fill you will every part of your being. It not only helps you mentally but physically also. Each time we are allowed to come through makes life easier for you. There will be a noticeable difference in your life and the things that you wish for start to happen. Consider us the genie in the bottle! As we have said, we are here for you. It is our greatest intent to help you.

When you have a problem or a question, we will be there to see if the help we offer will make all things better. It may be a word or a sign for you to watch for. Tinker loves the sounds of nature. She feels the beauty in it. We try our best to come in and, in a way, connect so she will understand and follow our lead to make her heart content. All life is there for you. Everything can be as it should. Try to be a part of it. Love all that is around you, even the smallest of the small.

Try to make a point of seeing the good. Once it has been seen, relish in it. Feel it to your core. Bask as much as you can. Believe us when we say it is all worth it!

Try to remember that love and life is all around you. Enjoy all that is given. Take nothing for granted. If you can connect and keep the positive flowing, everything will fall into place. When you feel this wonderful energy pass it on. Help others feel the same. Be in love with giving. As Tinker says, *Gratitude with Attitude*. Keep a smile of your face as much as possible. Being connected with your inner being is the most rewarding emotion that there is.

You will find that the connection will move forward to all that are around you. What a wonderful contagious thing it can be. To know that you and you alone have made others smile and enjoy life as much as you do. Be that person that when you enter anywhere you go; everyone is so glad that you are there! Just imagine it, you are the reason that they now are in the wonderful high vibration that they should be. You caused this for them. You are the one that they look forward to seeing.

As their day goes forward, they too will do the same as you did. Put a wonderful smile on others' faces that they meet during the day. It will become a regular way of living life. To be able to get up every morning and realize that all is good around you and them.

If there is a day that starts out not to be in the high vibration, convince yourself that this is not going to be your kind of day. Think positive thoughts and start imaging your day as another beautiful encounter. We promise that if you will start your day with a smile and outlook that everything is good, it will flow forward and end up being the way you want it to be.

Life on Earth is so worth living. That is why you are there. You chose to be a part of this that is happening now. Be what you came to Earth to be. Nothing is more important than being and seeing all that you can. You make a difference!

Shhhhhhhh!
There is wisdom within.
Listen!

www.BelieveAndCreate.com

Chapter V
Dreams vs. Visions

We all have them. They are there whether you realize it or not. That place in your mind that can take you places and do things you could never imaging while you're awake. The dream world is a time when you can be at peace with yourself. Your breathing is usually gentle and deep. The rhythm gives your mind a self-hypnotic focus.

If you don't remember your dreams, you are probably missing the most intriguing plots and mysteries that your mind can offer. They usually peak around 3 a.m. at the thinnest point of the veil. The place that is closest to here and the Other Side.

This is the where your subconscious actually speaks directly to you! Any upset or delightful thing that has happened the previous day you might take as just a way to shrug off whatever was going on. But, is it really doing that? There are sometimes messages that need to come through.

Your dreams are a way for you to communicate or find out what needs to be done to make your life right for yourself. Dreams can direct you to what may be happening in the future. Messages can be relayed from the Other Side in your dreams.

I've been told that our senses operate at three levels when we are in our dream state. There is the physical, the psychic, and the spiritual.

For years I read and kept up with Edgar Cayce's A.R.E. dream interpretation. There are loads of books and websites that you can investigate and get information. Edgar Cayce was a man that would go into a dream state and help others follow their way through his dreams. He could even help with healing and past life regression and interpretations.

His assistant kept a log of everything he said, which is now a library of all his teachings. Look into it. There are symbols and actions in your dreams that mean something.

For myself personally, my dreams are straight forward. Through a dream I was given the name of the younger of my Guys. Have yet to know the name of my old soul. Guess it's not for me to know currently.

You may want to keep a dream journal of all you have dreamt. It can help with working out the meaning of what has happened in your dreams. Keep it next to where you sleep and upon first waking up, jot down all that you can remember. It may not make sense at first but may prevail in what you need in the future. Read it later and see if there may be a message.

When the time comes that someone we know has passed to the Other Side and wants to talk and visit with us, in the dream it is very real. They may have a message or just want to connect.

My dad passed away when I was twenty-four years old. From that time, he never came to me at all! I would ask for him to visit but it didn't happen until I got pregnant with my first son.

The whole time I was pregnant he visited on a regular basis. The weird thing is, he never said a word—not one! He was there in the dream and would be with me and show me love, but not one word was spoken. This happened each time I got pregnant. I have three sons, and each time he was there, never uttering a sound. Once I gave birth to them, he was gone. No matter how much I asked him to come and visit with me, nothing!

Since then he has only visited one other time. My mind was set that, come hell or high water, he was going to visit me whether he liked it or not. (Remember how I told you earlier he was headstrong!) Over and over, I requested him to come through. Over and over, nothing. But I didn't give up.

Finally, one night, there he was. Seemed we were in a beautiful park setting and he was sitting near a pond with his old chair that he loved, smoking his pipe.

"Well, Daddy, it's about time. Why do you refuse to visit me?"

He took a long drag on his pipe, looked me in the eye and said this. "You've got this, Tinker. You don't need me to be here with you. I raised you to be the independent woman that you are. Now get back to what you were meant to do. Raise those boys of yours like I raised you. I'll be watching but just do what needs to be done."

That was it. He was gone and I woke up with a grin on my face. Not from his advice but from me being able to make him come through. *Now* who's the headstrong one?

Now let's talk about visions. Visions are exactly that. The direct way to go if there is any question. The teachings that I have read say that the way to tell the difference between a dream and a vision is in your vision state you remember every detail that went on. Every move or action that took place. It doesn't leave your memory at all! It seems to be permanently engraved in your mind.

One of my visions that I had was that I was focused on the shoes that I was wearing. Upon wearing these shoes, I received a promotion at work and was constantly wearing these shoes. They were brown wing tip business shoes with a three-inch heel. Thin black laces and they fit perfectly.

After having the vision, I immediately went looking for those shoes! Everywhere I looked, they just weren't there! I finally gave up. (Yeah, I was working against the flow, but I *so* wanted this promotion that I had busted my ass for.)

Kept working every day, but those shoes every now and then would pop into my head. It had been a while since the vision. I kept thinking maybe it was just a dream, with the symbol being the shoes. But I remembered every detail of what happened! It never left my mind.

Long story short, one day without even thinking about those shoes I went to the local Kmart to pick up a few things we needed at home. Walking down an isle there was a display of shoes on sale. Low and behold there they were! There were the exact shoes I had envisioned.

I scooped them up and brought them home. Couldn't believe that they were there and on sale too! Started wearing them on a regular basis and—you guessed it—I got that promotion in a matter of weeks.

Don't you just love when something like this happens? There were so many thank yous coming out of me for that one.

Another example is I had asked my Guys what the easiest way was to make it through life here on Earth. After a few days of this on my mind one night I began to dream.

I walked up to this large solid wooden door. It has a huge metal handle and upon opening it there was a very large room that was scarcely lit. At the back of the room was a table extended from one end of to the other. Sitting behind the table were Orthodox Jewish men. There had to be at least twenty-five of them lined up and sitting there just staring at me. My first thought was "Oh, shit!"

I slowly walked up to the table and asked them, "How can I make life easier for myself?" The guy right in front of me started to chuckle. Then they all started to chuckle and laugh. It proceeded into all of them letting out these loud, deep belly laughs.

The gentleman right in front of me said, "This is the secret: always laugh at everything! No matter what life deals out to you, be happy and laugh." With that, the dream ended.

If you look into the teachings of many Native American beliefs, they have many visions of what will be going on now and in the future. From my perspective it is probably because they are so in touch with our Mother Earth. I myself also try to be like this ever since I traipsed up that hill and got pulled back by that little dog.

There is a balance for us to follow. When you are connected to the other souls around you, it seems that you become aware of more in life. The souls I'm talking about aren't human souls! These are the souls of other living things that are just as much a part of our world as we are.

Here is something you can practice helping with getting in touch. May seem a little bizarre but just try it. Hug a tree. That's right, go out find you a nice big tree and hug it. Close your eyes and feel its life. There's a wonderful low humming vibration. For me, they have the most beautiful and precious energy that I have ever felt. It is a warm and steady energy. Just do it!

Message from my Guys

When all life was created on Earth, it was like a musical concert. Each and every person and thing was in harmony playing their part. There was life, love, and happiness. Every being understood their part and place. Each had their own initiative.

Since then, things have gotten out of balance. We in the non-physical want to help get back the balance and harmony. This is where you come in. You are the greatest love of the Creator. You are there to live and learn. To take on a challenge and make all things better. Through your great soul and understanding all is possible.

Let us together bring back the harmony that is missing. Be the guiding light that is required. See all that is possible. Love with all your heart, especially the Earth creatures that need you.

Life can be so grand for all. Feel the vibration in the Earth and follow it with all your heart and soul. You are the keepers. You are the ones that nurture the Earth. It is through you that all things are possible. Once again, be the light. Take the initiative to be involved in one way or the other. One simple act will cause another to happen. If the only thing you can do is pick up a piece of trash and deposit where it needs to be, then do it.

We cannot strive enough on how much you are needed. So many can make right the wrong with Earth. Make everything as it is meant to be. Let your heart guide you in whatever needs to be done. Follow your dreams and the signs they give you. You will know when it is time. Strive to be happy in your heart and soul. It is a simple act to follow.

If you put forth the effort to be in simplistic harmony,

you will notice a change in yourself. Things that are needed in your life will come to you without much trying on your part. It can be looked at like a gift for being what you were meant to be anyway.

With your imagination, anything is possible. The only thing that is needed is for you to get into that wonderful vibrational energy that is there for you to take advantage of. It is really a very simple thing to do. Don't try to make it harder than it is!

We in the non-physical are trying our best to guide you to that one point where you are meant to be. Please feel us there with you, feel us guiding you to your own beautiful vibration that has been waiting for you to dive into and make the difference for you and everything around you.

There is nothing purer and flowing as being on the ride of positive vibrational energy. We see on Earth those that ride this tide of energy without much effort. It is our place to try to get all to join into what is meant for you. The only thing that you really have to do is let it flow. Try by not trying; relax and let it happen. Close your eyes and feel it around you, circling and wanting to be a part of you.

Life can be so wonderful and fulfilling for all if you just let it happen! Let that pulsing energy like a heartbeat be a part of you. Soak it in like a bright sunny day. Feel it on you, around you, and in you. Once you have it there, you will never want to let it go!

There will be times that it may elude you, but once you have figured out how to connect it will take very little effort to re-establish the connection. One way is to imagine that it is an electrical current that you can plug into. Plug in and join it with all that you have. Become that bright light bulb that never dims. Light up the room for all to see.

Make others realize that life is grand, and it can be for them too.

When messages come through to you in your dreams and visions, pay attention to what is there to guide you. Let us know that you need us and in your dreams we can help. We can directly connect with you and tell you what you need to do. We can be one with you, all you have to do is ask us to please be there in your dreams.

If there is something that has appeared to us on the horizon that we feel you need to know, there will be a vision to guide you. It will come through with details that you cannot ignore. Use it and follow until it has come true. We are here, we are listening!

*When you don't know
how you know...
But you know you know...
And you know you knew
and that's all
you need to know...*

*Zen to Zany
@SpiritualAsylum*

Chapter VI
Intuition and Premonition

Have you ever had that feeling that you just *know* something? It's right there in front of your mind and you just know!

This happens all the time for me. There have been many times that I would tell one of my boys something and their reaction would be, "How do you know?"

My reply is, "I just know!"

From the time I was out playing and being a kid, I knew I would have three children. Never questioned it, I just knew. You get asked many times growing up, so how many children are you going to have, and I would always answer three.

The meaning of intuition is *the ability to understand something immediately without the need for conscious reasoning.*

The meaning of premonition is *a strong feeling that something is about to happen, especially something unpleasant.*

We all have this ability to be able without question have an answer before it is asked.

For instance: my writing this book. I knew it was time. My Guys would sometimes bring it up, but my question was, "Write a book about *what*?"

Then one day out of the blue it came to me, and here it is. Write about what you know, what you *really* know that will help others know too.

As I have said earlier in these pages, I'm one that

researches everything that sparks my interest. Needless to say, when this all started there was an immediate urge to look and see what goes into writing and publishing.

Because of algorithms, everything that you now pump into the all-seeing Google is immediately branched out to those that want to also see what you're doing.

What I am trying to do is be able to put what I know down in my own time to be sure that you as a reader get the full benefit.

Just this morning as I was leaving for work, this feeling of *something*, some inward emotional feeling, told me to be careful.

The way I travel is a side road with the speed limit of 30 miles per hour until I hit a main highway. Because of my feeling, extra caution was on my mind. I hadn't heard from my Guys, so I knew this was different.

As I was traveling there was a car coming towards me from the opposite direction. All of a sudden there she was: a small deer sprang out and tried to jump over the front of the car coming towards me. She looked to be a little older than a yearling. We both slammed on our brakes and the other car barely tipped her back left leg.

At that moment my heart went to my throat. I could feel her surprise and pain. I saw the spit come flying out of her mouth from the moment of surprise, and my thoughts where it was as much a surprise to her as it was to us.

I watched this poor animal fall and spin off the road. I sat for a moment to see if she was badly injured. She jumped right up and was gone in an instant, using the leg that was hit and headed for the woods.

The man that hit her was watching too. There didn't

seem to be any damage to his hood or front bumper, so she was just tapped by the car.

I could still feel her heart racing as I began to move again. Tears came to my eyes, which I pushed back.

This is perfect example of paying attention to your own premonitions. If I had been going much faster, I would have been the one to hit her and possibly kill her.

Where I live there is still plenty of woods and countryside, and the wildlife is abundant. Plenty of creatures live with us and being one of those that gives respect to nature and its inhabitants, this would have crushed me knowing I had cause another to leave this world in such a horrible way.

The next morning, she was there again at the side of the road at the same spot. This time there was no hurry to get across. She made herself noticeable from the side of the road and casually walked across. She had a slight limp but otherwise seemed okay. Also, she had a friend following her. Both little females made it across safely!

Here is another example of my intuition. In this one instant I can't decide if it is something everyone has or being a mom made the difference.

As I got up one morning and came into my living room, I felt something in the pit of my stomach. This ping, I guess you could call it, that someone I was close to was having some sort of trouble.

Immediately, the phone was in my hand and there were texts going out to my boys and close friends.

In about five minutes my eldest son texted me back and told me it was him. He had just received a call from his doctor. Seems his body had issues in creating enough testosterone among other things, so the poor guy must go on a regiment of self-injections until they can get a handle on it. Once he told me, the feeling went away.

There are a few things that you can hook into in your own self that may tell you that you are in touch with your intuition and premonition. Here is a pointer or two that can help make that connection.

Have time for solitude. If you are like me, there must be a time in the day that you want to be by yourself. My time is first thing in the morning. My brain takes a while to get moving when I first wake up, so I designate this to having peace and quiet time to connect with my deepest inner wisdom.

Some say that people with intuition and premonition are reclusive and inward. Can't say that I agree with this. My personality is very outgoing, and generally I'm a people person.

Here are some ways to get connected:

Try to always have a way of getting in touch with that gut feeling. This is a bridge between instinct and reason. Something like a hunch comes to your mind and you follow through on how you feel. There always must be a balance.

Be creative! At times you can see something in your mind, and before long you're working on it. Making it happen. Sometimes, you notice everything! You have a way of seeing things that are happening and notice how often they are coincidences, connections to your everyday life.

Your body speaks and you listen, just like the example I gave earlier. My body was telling me something. That *gut instinct* came through.

Connect deeply with others. This is empathy. Just like

that poor deer; I felt what she was feeling. Maybe you see someone that has been embarrassed and you *feel* that embarrassment.

A lot of this can come through dreams! They can play a big role in being connected to both your intuition and premonition. When you dream, your brain is receiving information from the unconscious part of the mind.

Enjoy the downtime that you have. There is nothing like having time to contemplate. Pull yourself away from that damn smartphone and enjoy just being you.

Don't let negative emotions affect you. It doesn't matter what anyone else thinks. All that matters are you and your wellbeing. Nothing will tear you apart more than dwelling on what may have been said to you or about you. Accept it and let it go!

Now you're probably asking, "Will this help me get in touch with my own personal Guys?" Sure it will! Please realize that the more you are in tune with your own gifts, the more they can communicate with you. Your ability to go within yourself only opens the door wider for them to get in touch. My Guys have always been there for me and yours have been there for you too.

From the moment that you were born they were there to see you through the veil and make sure that you took your first breath. From what I understand, there is great rejoicing every time a child is born. It is one more that the Creator has made, and he looks forward to the accomplishments that can be had through that one physical being.

When my boys were born, there was a feeling that they could make a difference on this Earth. They were given to me to raise and the Creator trusted me to do the best that

I could for them. I tried my best to do just that. They have grown up to be strong, independent, and thoughtful young men.

Each one of them have been taught to pay attention to all that is around them. To zero in on that is there and be in tune with what is going on with them. There are times that they have shared a premonition with me and asked what my thoughts were about it. It makes me feel honored that they value what my outlook might be.

Once you start a regular routine of doing what your intuition tells you, life gets easier! There isn't so much doubt in your mind. You become more sure of yourself.

Message from my Guys

You are blessed with these wonderful emotions and feelings. To be able to see from within yourself and put it forward to work for you. This is the point where we can come in and help with whatever decision that you may want to make. You in the physical world are so much more capable that you realize. Your soul works for you nonstop and is there always help from us if you so demand. Whether you realize it or not, during your stay on Earth, you are still connected with the non-physical. That is why when you go within, we can connect with you. You never really truly totally leave from here on the Other Side of the veil. A part of you stays and there is the connection between you and us. It is like a small, connected ribbon that runs between the physical and non-physical. This is the great unconditional love that exists between all creatures that are now there.

Here is a thought. If you have a connection with a pet that you know truly loves you, this is the example of what true unconditional love is. They never tire of you, always are there for you and would never leave your side. They are a perfect example of the way that all of you should be. With this connection of another creature, it gives you the practice and example on how to improve your connection with us. They too have a life to live and they also strive to be able to cross over the veil knowing that what they did was the right thing, and yes, they are waiting for you when your time comes to cross over! This is a way to look and learn from others. It doesn't have to be your own species to be able to see how to connect.

This is how we connect with you. It is unconditional love that makes all things possible. We are here, just like your favorite pet. In the non-physical world, that is what keeps us so in tune with positive vibrational energy. Unconditional love is what leads us to do what is right for you and everything around you.

Just like your favorite pet, we patiently wait for you to walk through that door into the alignment of positive energy. With the power you have in intuition and premonition, it brings us one step closer to helping you. All we ask is that you pay attention and follow what lead is given. You know the difference between right and wrong, so use what you are intended to use. It is there for you.

We cannot begin to tell you how much you can achieve just by paying attention and becoming aware. Everything flows to you. Become the wave that you were meant to be. Connect and become! Strive and let your light shine through. We are waiting just behind that door; open it and let us shower you with all that we have!

What we are trying to say is that everything is just a

positive thought. If you expect it and in turn accept it, your whole being will vibrate into what it is that you truly need. When you visualize, we see what it is that you are trying to accomplish. We push forward and put out signs and signals that will make it real.

You will not become abundant or have prosperity by making a decree over and over, but you will come to realize that you are spiritual, and this is your nature to constantly increase the flow of energy vibration. You can increase your awareness, which in turn will increase your flow to and from any and all substance. The more awareness that you put into it, the more will appear. It all comes from within you!

*Reincarnation is essential
to enable the soul
to evolve to
its Divine right.*

R. F. Goudey

Chapter VII
Reincarnation and Karma

Reincarnation is the act of coming forth again and again until we get it right. This is the whole of our existence. To be the best we can possibly be and return to our Divine as the perfect spark that he gave us to live.

There is a quote that hits home for me.

Reincarnation is the law of spiritual evolution. It gives everything a chance to work out its Karma (the law of action). The method of propelling all creation towards final freedom of spirit, held no longer under natural law of death. —Paramahansa Yogananda

From what I understand from all my research and personal experience on this subject, it is up to us whether we stay on the Other Side or come back to physical form if that's what we truly desire.

The overall question is: Do you want to take a full head plunge into another round of festivities and pure pleasures, or do you want to develop your spiritual side? If you choose the latter, are you willing to help others advance that are in the physical? This is a group thing, as I have told you earlier! Everyone must take part in the advances only as all move upward toward the common goal of enlightenment and perfection.

The only ones that don't get this option are ones that have committed great horrendous acts against others. This is the true sin. Then, the soul will lay idle for a long period time unless there is a lot of evil in its nervous being, then it can return to trouble those that are in the physical.

Ever heard of being haunted? Well, there it is! The troubled ones that seem not to let go of this side because of what they are accustomed to dealing out.

There is a personal experience I have on this. The father of my three sons passed a few years back. We had been together for twenty years. He ended up being very narcissistic and abusive both physically and verbally. Bad alcoholism seemed to push him over the edge. We had not been together for about a year when he passed. There was a restraining order against him seeing the boys, and he felt I was to blame for that.

Once he moved to the Other Side, it didn't take long for him to come through and try to make my life miserable again. He even took control of a black bird that would sit on my shepherd's hook outside my living room window and stare at me in the living room. This poor bird would sit from daylight to dusk. This went on for months.

He was constantly trying to get in my head and tell me what a horrible mother I was. Even my dog saw him in the house and would growl at him each time he appeared.

Finally, one day when I was backing out of my driveway, he started coming through and telling me once again what a horrible mother I was and proceeded to emphasize it. Feeling a little enraged, I finally told him to shut the hell up and leave me and the boys alone. Immediately after, I heard my Guys laughing hysterically.

My next words were this. "Dammit, Guys, quit laughing and take care of this! Please don't allow him to come around us again! *I mean it!* Make him stop." They went silent. From that moment on, it was a little quieter around the house. No more awful visits, the dog settled down, and the black bird finally left.

There are times that the soul doesn't realize that he has passed and at that moment they hover around everyone wondering why no one seems to pay attention to him or her on the physical side. Other times they will make a deliberate return because they can't seem to give up thoughts of having worldly goods and possessions.

As for myself, when my time comes, I'm ready. Knowing that there truly is no death and I live on from this plane to another is enough for me. Deep down there is this knowing of everlasting. Mine is an old soul. There are memories of different lives, and I can remember two vividly; others are touch and go.

There is and always has been a great love for Earth inside of me. Seems each time I'm here there is a wanting to help in any way possible. Now more than ever she needs all the help she can get.

But, back to the subject at hand. The first life I remember is being in Lemuria. Yes, I was a Lemurian. For those that aren't familiar with this lost land, here's a breakdown.

Lemuria was a huge land mass that was located in the Pacific Ocean. The only remains of it are Hawaii and the Fiji Islands. Many don't believe there was such a place, but I do because I was there. It existed around the same time as Atlantis.

The Lemurians were the keepers of the crystals and balance with nature. There are visions in my head of being taught the significance of always taking care of our Earth.

There is one memory of my standing in a doorway arch made of huge gray stones looking out and seeing small palm trees with a gentle tropical breeze blowing. Listening closely, I could hear the ocean in the distance.

My clothes were made of a gauze type material. They hung loosely down to the floor. My hair was long and dark.

There was a woman that was a type of high priestess that was the teacher and keeper of knowledge. We were constantly learning of our world and the importance of keeping it alive and beautiful.

Our city was made of stone; to me it looked like a type of limestone. There were buildings lining a walkway made of earth with running water trenches on both sides of the walkway. The walkway led to a larger building at the end. This is where I lived. Apparently, I was in training to be one of the priestesses.

I had a room in which I slept, all made of stone. To my left as I was lying in my bed was an opening like a huge window or entrance to a small balcony, that had the same type of gauze that I wore across its entrance. I have memories of watching the gauze dance in the wind as I laid in bed, smelling the wonderful scents that danced in my room from outside.

Another memory of this time is of my sitting on a log and finding a skull at my feet. Upon picking up the skull, I held it in between my hands and started gently stroking the cheek bones as I blew soft breaths on its face. Before long, this skull started to take shape and as I worked my fingers down blowing soft breaths upon its being, it came to life. This creature was a beautiful dark red fox.

Once life was returned to this beautiful being, we sat watching each other for a few moments, then he proceeded to slowly walk away, looking back at me from time to time. The feeling of love and compassion came over me knowing that I had helped a wonderful creature live again.

You may be wondering how I know this. Well first, I'm an old fart and have many years of putting this all together! And second, once you start getting in touch with your inner self, you will too.

Below is a list that will help you to see if there are signs that you may have been missing to let you know you have reincarnated.

Recurring dreams. They keep happening over and over. It seems that you remember in what another life was like. Many children have these and often tell their parents of being someone else.

Out of place memories. You know that you remember a place or time, but it just doesn't coincide with your now.

You have a strong intuition. This goes back to the "I know that I know" without knowing *how* you know!

Déjà vu. The strong feeling that this has happened before or that you have been there before without actually being there.

Empathy. To be able to *feel* everything. A consciousness of what others are going through.

Precognition. Yes, that feeling in the pit of your stomach that something is about to take place without knowing exactly what it is.

Retrocognition. The knowledge of knowing something has taken place in the past without any memory of how you know.

Feeling older than your age reflects. Having a knowledge of life as if you have been here for ages and ages.

Having a great affinity for certain cultures, periods of time, or environments. A connection with the ability to know for certain that moments in time did take place and you were there to witness it.

Unexplainable fears or phobias. Always having a fear of something without being able to explain why. For instance, fear of water means you may have drowned in a past life.

Feeling as though this Earth in not your home. The realization of knowing you were born here but deep down there is a longing of somewhere else. A place that you can really call home.

Each one of these on this list can help you reach a point of understanding that you have been here before.

Another life I remember is a time back when St. Francis of Assisi was alive. We were childhood friends. I have a memory of us playing together as children on the cobble stone streets and looking up and seeing olive trees on the hills as we played. We both came from prominent families in the town where we lived. The memory of his leaving to be who he became, and more than likely my great love of animals.

Seems through the lives I remember being here on this lovely planet there has always been that love for the Earth and all its creatures. Earth has always been my home, so on the list of different things the last one doesn't pertain to me. Could be because I was a Lemurian; they were the first beings to inhabit Earth.

Now, to dive into Karma. Oh, how this can bite you right square in your back side! The law of cause and effect. To quote I've heard for many years, "*Karma is a bitch only if you are!*"

Karma is the understanding of our identity as souls, our oneness of being spiritual beings who were created by the Divine. As sparks of the Creator, we are held accountable for what we create, promote, or allow in our lives. As mentioned in previous pages, it is all a balancing act. It is our responsibility to do what is right or pay our debt for not doing so.

This thing called Karma isn't physical—it's definitely spiritual—but we as souls also carry Karma forward through time in this life and the next. It plays out in our life now through our thoughts, feelings, circumstances, relationships, and (last but not least) experiences. The main game in the physical world is to pay it off as a debt rather than adding up new ones so we can know ourselves and others as the Divine beings and be able in the long run to enter into the consciousness of the Creator.

Here are some really easy ways to build up good Karma now so it can become a habit. It's always better to be nice!

Offer a compliment. It doesn't hurt you to look at someone and offer a nice gesture towards them. Say something positive like "Love the new shoes" or "Great job."

Always say thank you! No matter what or how minor it is. Having a habit of getting breakfast in the morning, I always give the drive-thru people a thank you when they hand me my order. It doesn't hurt and I'm sure it helps them with dealing with the public. Even with my boys, no matter what they may do for me I always say thank you.

Listen to someone. Sometimes it's better to say nothing at all. There are times when people just need someone that they can just talk to. Take the time to help them by being a sounding board.

Show up. If you have decided to meet someone and be somewhere with them, go! Whether the weather turns crappy, you've had a bad day, or life really sucked the past few hours, show up anyway. It shows that you are a reliable person and you actually care.

Be a teacher. There are times that someone may not know how to do something. It could be something really simple, but they haven't ever had to do it. Help them and be a teacher. Don't roll your eyes; do it with a smile and let them know you were happy to help.

Let go of past bad experiences. This is a big one! Old baggage never helped anyone. Let it go and move on. It's not going to help you at all to keep contemplating in the past. You're better than that! Remember earlier in the book about going with the flow? Quit trying to go against the current.

Rid yourself of toxic people. You know the ones, always negative, always have something bad to say about everything. Try to move away from this. It doesn't do you or your soul any good to jump on their bandwagon and fuel the fire. With enough hatred and bad things going on around us, try to look at the more positive things and be that person.

Knock it off with the ego. No one is better than anyone else. It's okay to be proud of yourself especially when you have used it to help others but keep the boasting of what all you've done to make yourself look better in someone else's is just so UGH! It really doesn't give you any brownie points in the whole scheme of things.

If you try to work at this every day, you will find that for some odd reason you feel better! Imagine that, feeling better by just being a nice person. Yes, there will be times that you must take a few steps back. It's normal in this day and time. But just be aware of what is happening and work yourself back up to that wonderful soul that you are.

Message from my Guys

When your life started again on Earth, there were certain debts that you carried forward to try to relinquish while you are there. Each and every person has their own karmic subjects and instances to work through to become better with each visit on Earth.

We on this side of the veil have our own debts too. Working with Tinker is one that we are working out so we can become what we need to be.

As we have said before through the millennium of time, it is all a balance. To be able to have the scale of creation even with no tilts to one side or the other. We have heard those on Earth say that there is no such thing as perfection. The answer to that statement is: yes, there is.

Even your pets that you have had through the years are working out their own way to be better, as all creatures are. They too must go back and forth from physical to non-physical. Some have been with you before in the life that you now have. We here on this side and you all in the physical are working for the same goal.

Through the whole process, the Divine is feeling each part of this. This is the goal for all: feeling and being balanced. This does not mean that you cannot have fine things as you go through your life on Earth. But you have a balanced consciousness that is centered in the ever-present substance of the Divine.

As you learn what to or not to do you will find that things will come easily as they are needed. Please read the sentence before with the keywords: *as they are needed*! In the world beyond the veil, we with our Divine have no substances such as cars, or homes, or luxury items that pull us away from our purpose. We realize where you are at this moment there are material things constantly being broadcast to you.

We know how easily all of this can be dominating your thoughts and how hard you may strive to get them. There is always something else to yearn for. Sometimes you feel the emptiness and need to try to fill it.

The secret is trying to build on what is right and filling in your life with the good Karma that is there for you. Strive to build on your awareness and expand on the inner wholeness. By practicing this you are expanding, and the things will come to you with abundance! Be aware that this abundance comes from your expansion. Let your uniqueness attract and manifest what you want in your life. All things are possible when you set forth and believe it will happen.

Try to keep in touch with us and with your will and belief you will see yourself start to grow and improve with each day. When you keep the creative flow going within you, there will be lessons learned which fills in the Karma and you will notice prosperity starting to flow towards you.

No miracles are required. This is the way you were created. You are a creative spiritual being. You can never be less than what you can be! Within yourself is the unborn possibility of a limitless stability and progressive experience coming forward. Everything is a privilege of giving life expansion from here, if you believe.

Try to have the ability to view everything from the top. Keep yourself centered and always have gratitude. There is Divine order in everything that happens in your life. Always remember it can be so much more. Continue to relish in your blessings, which in turn will lead you towards the prosperity that is waiting for you.

Identify yourself with substance that is there for you. As this comes through, good Karma is abundant, and you can start to rejoice in the ever-present Divine blessings that you have been waiting for!

*In order for the light
to shine so brightly,
the darkness must be present.*

Sir Francis Bacon

Chapter VIII
Good vs. Evil

Since the beginning of man, this has been the one and only thing that has been consistent. It has always been good versus evil. To know the difference and to be able to do something about it.

Here's a breakdown. To be good is to show a lack of self-centeredness. This is the ability to empathize with other people and feel at some point compassion for them. To try to put their needs before ours.

Sometimes it is necessary to sacrifice your own wellbeing for the sake of others. To have benevolence and selflessness and to be able to sacrifice towards a greater cause. This is the empathy that all should feel for others. To be able to see beyond the difference of race, gender, or nationality and to be able to see the common human essence between them.

All those people in history that are now considered "saintly" have these fine qualities in abundance. Martin Luther King Jr. and Mahatma Gandhi are examples of those that risked their own wellbeing and safety for the purpose of gaining equal rights and freedom for everyone. These two while in the physical had an exceptional degree of empathy and compassion, which overcame any concern for their own ambitions or wellbeing.

On the other hand, to be evil are those who are unable to empathize with those around them. Their own desires and needs are more important. They tend to be selfish, have huge egos, and are self-absorbed and generally narcissistic. It's usually the case that their only value for others is to help themselves satisfy their own desires and to exploit each person that crosses their path. This can be seen in the life of Hitler, as his primary characteristic was to take advantage of others for his own goals.

They can't sense other's emotions or suffering. There is no clue in their mind for other people's perspectives and have no sense of their rights. Everyone to them is strictly there to be used as objects, which makes their brutality and cruelty possible.

This also applies to serial killers and rapists. They don't see what they are doing as wrong. The need to fulfill their own desires is their first priority, and this is their main goal.

Most of us lie in between the two extremes. We have days that we behave badly, when there are impulses in us that cause us to put our needs before the welfare of others. Then there are times that we behave more in an empathetic nature and compassion compels us to put the needs of those around us before our own.

Guess the main point here is when we try to be a good person, to help our fellow human beings, there seems to be a connection. Having this connection often shows a fundamental necessity to be as one with human nature. We are all sparks of the Divine, made of the same elements.

Evil seems to be a departure from the normal. Set oneself aside from all others, which in the long run cripples the personality, and what emerges is being broken off and disconnected, fragments of what should be.

This evil isn't necessarily what we call the devil, but the vibrations that come from those that have gathered force through the moments in past and present. Each wrongdoing gathers strength just as good shines forth with each thoughtful deed.

This all began from the beginning of us as physical beings. The Divine energy put forth in us to be good and decent souls, but there were those that when inhabited with the physical life they needed to fight, squabble, and lust, hoping to enhance their own importance. This is where we as humans were given free will. It was our choice to be one or the other. By these actions this established an energy force which in the moments of time built up and became the evil we know today. (Hold on to your hats, I'm about to go there!)

This may be a shock to you, but **man** created evil, not the Divine. So, we as human beings created what we refer to as Satan, which is fed each and every moment by every terrible thought and action, twenty-four hours a day, 365 days a year.

People make the comment, "How can God let this happen?" But God *didn't* let this happen, we did! It's not up to our Divine Creator, it is up to us! You know, the free will thing I just talked about. The Divine put us here to be able to feel what we feel. Earlier in this book I emphasized that the main point is to feel good and happy because that's what the Divine wants to feel through us. But with our actions, those negative vibrational energies are going outward just as much as the good. Therefore, you get what you get. If you want better things in this life, you must put out that positive, beautiful energy in order to receive it back plus more.

In order to rid ourselves of this negative ripple that seems to be growing each and every day and to be able to destroy the negative what we have created, we need to *wake up!* We as beings in physical form need to push our awakening and realize that even thoughts and deeds of being a better human can shrink the size of evil by each moment, we replace an ugly thought or action with loving kindness.

Upon doing this, we can approach an infinite future where good can replace evil in the hearts of those who still relish and wallow in it. Follow by example, make every effort to put that best foot forward in whatever comes to play in your life.

The more you connect to your soul the more of the awareness will come through. This will enable you to live a more meaningful life, not just for yourself but for those around you and for our Divine.

Message from my Guys

We in the non-physical watch this plague of non-connectedness, and it is something that can be pushed back with help. Each and every person has a choice. A choice to be awake and live each day as a gift of a new beginning. It is our greatest and best desire to see all of you in a happy light. In order to do this, you must step forward and make the effort to shine.

The Earth can be full of so much love and abundance, it would shake your core to see what we see. There is so much more if you in the physical would take the moment to connect and make the difference. Every want that you can imagine could come forward and your life could be the bliss you desire.

The main way to do this is be happy! No matter what is going on tell yourself that it is going to get better. Believe in yourself, make the conscious effort to see a rainbow after the storm. We promise that if you can do this every day, your life will be bright and have meaning.

With this action you will see a difference in the actions of others. They too will begin to smile and show the happiness within. It is like a beautiful disease that can be so contagious.

Please make the effort to shine and see the beauty in everything. Life will change for you, that is a fact.

*And then it happens...
One day you wake up
and you're in this place.
You're in this place where everything feels right.
Your heart is calm.
Your soul is lit.
Your thoughts are positive.
Your vision is clear.
You're at peace, at peace with where you've been,
at peace with what you've been through,
and at peace with where you're headed.*

Unknown

Chapter IX
Time for your Awakening!

Sometimes you may ask yourself, "What in the hell am I doing?" This question may become more frequent the longer you breathe and notice the actual world around you. Did you ever think that this moment in your physical self is the actual moment that you are awakening?

The more that you make a connection with what is going on in your life, the more you'll question your very being, and it's usually an indication that you have realized it is time to wake up! The moment that you start connecting with your soul is the moment you experience a transformation. This causes you to have a true taste of joy, peace, fulfillment, and freedom.

We all have this presentation in life when you just know that it is time to connect to a more spiritual way of doing things. The sensation of what you are doing doesn't make sense anymore. This is because your former beliefs and desires are challenged and many times disproven.

This awakening can happen at any moment and at any time. It can be spontaneous, but it can also be set off by a major life change: tragedy, illness, divorce, an accident, anything that can jolt you in to thinking that there must be more.

There may be moments that you feel completely disconnected from everything around you and that includes your spiritual beliefs. You must go through darkness before you see the light. If you find yourself very sensitive to the suffering of those around you and there are moments of deep thinking, it is possible that you are having or well on your way to be at the point of awakening.

Believe me, I've been there! It can be the most grueling treacherous feelings that can come together at one time. Confusion, to put it lightly! You feel as though you're in a deep pit and can't imagine a way out.

What I want to do is to break it down for you. There is no *actual* step by step procedure, but here and now you can read and understand that you aren't losing it, you're just getting ready for something that is going to completely blow you away! So here we go, get ready!

Stage 1: You feel lost and unhappy. You are searching for something and you really don't know what it is. You feel empty. The depression can be so unbearable—a disconnection is taking place, and you can't fix it.

Stage 2: There is a moment when everything starts looking like there is a different way regarding reality. There is an awareness that you are unhappy with the way things are going. It disturbs you to see suffering, it eats at you of all the ills in the world. You start looking at life in a different way.

Stage 3: This is when you start looking at something deep inside you an inward vision of yourself. You begin to start asking through your thoughts all these deep questions that had never crossed your mind before. There is now a searching for a life's purpose. You know and realize that there is a *feeling* of what really is the meaning of life. There is a need to find help in any form you can put your hands on: metaphysical, esoteric, and self-help information to find the answers and truths.

Stage 4: At this moment is where there is all the soul

searching. Feelings of connecting to some teachers or maybe a belief system that can end this suffering that you are now going through. Your life feels as if it is expanding and some of those old patterns that you had followed earlier seem to be dissolving. A sense of true self begins to show on the horizon. There may be moments of unexplained experience or periods of enlightenment that give you a small glimpse into the actual nature of your reality. This is the moment of *awe*! Now there is a joy, hope, and connection that you have searched for your entire life.

Stage 5: Hold on! You're not quite there yet. In physical form it is all about movement. Remember the flow of water? In this stage, you begin to realize that there is a type of boredom from the spiritual teachers and all the practices. There is a huge amount of fake spiritual bull crap out there and currently you have a craving for something much deeper. You may have experienced periods of connection with the Divine. This connection will flow in and out of you, and thus experiencing this upset will only help you to be pulled back in. This is normal! This can be very disturbing, but hang in there. This craving for authenticity and for the deep spirituality that can transform every part of you is moving forward. This lull and unhappiness that you feel at these moments will motivate you to get out there and search for more.

Stage 6: With this stage coming forward, you are no longer interested in the feel-good dabbling with spiritual philosophies for those just touch the surface practices that are so abundant. The seeking you feel inside motivates you to go deeper and get going on the inner work. This is when you become the student of mindfulness and meditation and have a yearning for ritual in order to get back in touch with that inner child that longs to come forward.

Stage 7: Now at this point, you take these lessons that have pushed your soul into a spiritual mental process and applying them to your everyday life. This process of incorporating yourself into equals of our society. Where you see yourself in different groups and you are aware that we are all slices of the whole. Now you will feel that beautiful profound connection and this gives you that long-lasting change deep within yourself. Periods of unity with the Divine comes forward and the self-realization that nothing is guaranteed, but there is a push to make it so. This is the true gift of life, to feel the peace, love, and joy. You may want to go forward and try to make a difference in your community or just be a mentor and pass this on to others. It's not all about you anymore but more about *we* and *us*. The big picture emerges, and you feel connected and at peace and are aligned with all that comes your way.

Stage 8: Here is the ultimate test as to whether you can stay on this path or get pulled back into that conundrum that sent you here in the first place. Life is full of curve balls and lessons to be learned. Remember what all you went through to get here. Keep in mind that there is always that flow. There will be times that you move back and then move forward. It's not a straight path but one that curves and twists for you to follow and remember this is always a process that is unique to you. Once you have gotten through all the steps, you know what it takes to keep moving in that wonderful, beautiful movement that makes life worth living!

When you reach this point things will look different to

you. Air will feel vibrant in your lungs. Colors in nature will be more vivid. It seems your hearing is more acute. There will be this awareness of everything around you. At times you seek the same in people's faces. You look at them and you can tell that they are aware too! Your vibration has changed, and others can pick up on that energy. We are one. We understand what others do not.

The best part that I like about this point of being aware is the bull crap that is thrown at you comes through loud and clear. You can tell from the moment they open their mouth the sound is not the energy that flows with what you have inside you.

Now life has a true meaning! Bask in it, bathe in the wonderful knowledge that has come to you finally in full form. Enjoy each and every part of your being because it is well worth it. Life is worth living!

This is an important moment! You are now at the point of you being where the great truth and discovery is at your beck and call. It isn't about the things that happen around you or things that happen to you, but the most important thing which is what really counts and that is the thing that happens inside of you. There is little control over the elements or the fluctuation of news and the markets or how someone may act. But the great thing now is you control the thoughts of your mind. It isn't always easy, but it is possible!

There are ideas that come to you and you can be the magnet that over and over again draws people, things, and certain circumstances to follow according to your thoughts. You realize your abundance begins with you. Now you can become synchronized with the energy flow, which in turn has the influence on you like walking outside and the bright sun hits you. It can be blinding, but you bask in it and welcome the flow of energy.

This has nothing to do with miracles, and don't look at it that way. Look back at the steps you went through to get here. Keep it in the back of your mind that everything around you will have an influence good or bad, but it is up to you and how you will deal with what is going on at that particular moment.

When you oversee your thoughts and you are in the oneness of that energy flow, to be able to remain optimistic regardless of what may be going on, you and only you change your luck. This is the point of moving towards your dreams. This is nothing more than Divine law.

This is where that boundary has been passed and you can work at it and interpret what your own outcome will be. Things will start working in your favor.

Once you start seeing the difference in how your life is changing, try to always look back and see how your gratitude has moved forward. There never needs to be a reason to be grateful and you don't need something to be grateful for. Just realize that you only need the desire to *feel* grateful. With that you become great and will attract great things. It all goes hand in hand.

Message from my Guys

We love to see this last step in the process of your being everything you wish to be. Our energy in the non-physical is beaming! It shows us that there is still hope and we are doing what we need to do from this side of the veil.

We relate to you. You realize that we are here and together we make it all worthwhile. We love seeing you with a lively step. Your smile is our smile. This is our whole purpose.

For years we watched Tinker go back and forth. She would connect and then disconnect. We in the non-physical would push for her to be the true light that she needed to be. Sometimes she would shine so bright and other times she had her clouds.

You will have these moments too. But after being awakened and connected, to see what was there and now missing at this point, there is a need to get back to that. Nothing is the same until you get the energy that made you whole, and this makes us shine with pride!

To quote what we have heard on Earth, "You are our everything." It gives us such great pleasure to see so many realizing that there is so much more. We love to see each and every one of you beaming and gleaming and dancing.

Tinker loves music. When she is connected there is so much music! We bask in her feeling the rhythm and the smile that comes across her face. She laughs, and there is so much joy all around her. She beams like a bright star.

We want this for all of you. We want to see the great beauty that comes forward. With this, the negative is pushed back more and more. It is what you are there to do. Please make this your one goal. To feel as though there is no ending to you and what you can do. You are each a spark of the Divine. When you feel this so do we. The Divine relishes this. We all relish this. You will see things happening for you so easily. Hardly any effort is needed to accomplish whatever you may need.

Keep working at this with all that you have. We will do our best to remove any obstacles that may be ahead of you on your path. Listen as much as you can to the voices you hear! No matter what, try to begin each morning with a smile and tell yourself it is going to be another wonderful day.

There is always a light to guide you. Be aware of your feelings and hopes every day. Look for the good in everything that happens. This is like a beacon to guide you to more and more abundance and prosperity. If there is a thought that comes to you and you feel the need to follow, please do. It was put there for a reason. You will know if it is something that you need to dive into. Pay attention to the wonderful feeling inside. If it is a good feeling follow it; if not, put it to one side and keep striving.

*Look deep into nature
and you will understand
everything better.*

Albert Einstein

Chapter X
Nature: the Drug of Choice

Today we live in a world that has become greedy and thinks of nothing more than profit with quick results. These actions play a major roll on the balance of our beautiful world. Not only is the way now polluted but there is stimulation of all those negative vibrations that I covered earlier. No matter how subtle, this plays a large role on our precious Earth. The negativity expands again and again to make everything a form of misery and violence.

This chapter is very close to my heart. I have had a great love for our Earth ever since I took that little traipse up the hill into the woods with my little dog. Growing up in a rural area didn't help any! There is a closeness there for me that at times can't be put into words. But this is about how to get you in sync with all that our Earth has to offer.

In ancient times, we as humans lived in balance between us and our surroundings. If we cut a tree down, it was replaced with many more. It is all about being equal. To be able to live with all creatures and everything that goes with it.

Nature had its own way to make the balance work. Think of it this way, there are five elements that form the basis and works to stabilize each other. The elements are fire, water, air, earth, and ether (space or spirituality). Water is everything that is liquid, air is all that is gas. Fire is that part of nature that transforms one state of matter to another. Ether is the mother of the other elements and is the basis of our higher spiritual experiences whether it is us or the creatures that we live with.

All of creation as we know it is made up of these five elements, of course in different proportions. Here is a breakdown of our human body, which has percentages of all five: water at 72%, earth at 12%, air at 6%, fire at 4%, and the rest is ether. For the most part, the first four elements remain constant, but the percentage of ether can be enhanced. This is where the spiritual connection comes in.

Each element is responsible for the structures in our physical form. Earth is responsible for teeth, nails, bones, muscles, skin, tissues, and hair. This is our strength. Water forms saliva, urine, semen, blood, and sweat. Fire forms hunger, thirst, sleep, and vision in our eyes, and it also determines the complexion of our skin. Air's responsibility is our movement, including expansion, contraction, vibration, and suppression. Finally, ether—the most subtle of the elements—is present in the hollow cavities of the body and is responsible for the cosmic rays, frequencies, light radiation, and vibrations.

There is an intimate connection between we as humans and the environment around us. Through history all of nature—mountains, rivers, sun, trees, and the moon—has always been honored in our ancient cultures. It's only when we started moving away from our connection to nature and ourselves that the beginning of pollution and the destroying of our environment started to take place.

Recently while on Facebook, a guy that I have known since he was in diapers was voicing his opinion about climate change. From the conversation I read, he doesn't believe it's happening. Could or couldn't be, but for me it's more of the energy around us that influences this action.

A few days later on social media, he made a post asking what has happened to all the whip-poor-wills. This is a tiny bird that calls out in the evening and night. It sounds just like its name. He hadn't heard them in a while, and this is when I chimed in.

My question back to him in the comments was, "What has happened to our beautiful whip-poor-wills?" At that point I included in my post the research being done, and it showed how they were starving to death. I furthered my comment by asking, "What has happened to all the bugs we had? How long has it been since you had to clean the bugs off your windshield?" So, to this I also added, "Well, the answer is our 4G phones. They are killing the bugs, which is starving the birds! It's all about balance!" He liked my comment but nothing else was said.

We can't destroy one without affecting the other, which in turn affects us. After all is said and done, we need to be able to experience our world with an open mind and heart. Being ourselves in physical form, we need to be aware of our own stress, which affects everything around us. Once we become calmer, we need to create the means of protecting our beautiful Earth. For this to happen, the human consciousness must rise above all greed and exploitation. Spirituality and having the connection to all that is around us can give the experience of one's own being deep within and provides the key to a vital relationship within oneself, with others, and with nature.

This connection to our own essential beings can and will eliminate negative emotions, elevate consciousness, and create a spirit of care and commitment for the planet as a whole.

So now you're asking, "How can I do this?" The answer is easy! Wherever you are, no matter what, go out and just be with nature. Where I am, it's not a problem, but there must be a place where you are that has trees, birds, grass, and blue skies: a park or even the small section of land that has been sitting vacant.

The easiest way that I have found to connect is to listen. Close your eyes and connect to the sounds of nature. Every morning as the sun comes up, I listen for birdsong. It is always at first light. There is such a harmony and wonderful melody that their wonderful voices throw out. Our lovely, winged friends can sing a beautiful and enticing song that can relieve any bad or stressful vibration you may be going through.

Every chance you get, take your shoes off and feel the Earth underneath you. Dig your toes in and *feel* what there is to offer. That warmth has the most giving vibration that you could ever imagine.

There is a film on YouTube that is free to watch called *The Grounded*. It's about a man that realized there was something to this idea and proved it to himself and others in the area where he lived in Alaska. Take the time to watch it if you want to learn what all of our connections can be with our beautiful world and all it has to offer.

There is also a personal experience that I need to share with you. This episode in my life proved to me that no matter what you can pull through anything that life throws at you.

At the beginning of 2015, I became very sick with a stomach flu. No matter what I tried to do, it just wouldn't get any better. I resisted going to the doctor because I had no insurance. The Great Recession had hit and the job I had for nearly twelve years was taken away. Needless to say, everything I tried didn't work.

Finally, in July of 2015 I reached a point and realized I was at the beginning of the end. That morning, I was unable to get off the couch. Called a friend of mine and asked for help to get me to the hospital.

She was there in a matter of minutes, but between her and my youngest son, they couldn't get me up; I was just about lifeless. Thank goodness she stepped up to the plate and called for an ambulance.

I was taken to a hospital in Nashville and admitted directly into the ICU. My oxygen level was between 86% and 88%, whereas normal is around 95%. One of my lungs had collapsed and the other was full of pneumonia. My liver was shot and I had fluid around my heart. Spent four days in the ICU before they moved me to a regular isolated room. It took two weeks for them to finally let me go home. I lost sixty pounds and there was barely anything left of me.

The thought in my mind the whole time this was happening was, "I don't have time for this!" This was not part of my plan. It never crossed my mind that death was an option.

While in the ICU my oldest son came in and was shocked by the sight of me. I looked like someone that had just come out of one of Hitler's concentration camps. He told me later that while driving to the hospital there were tears in his eyes because he was thinking that now he was losing the other parent. Then, he said, it hit him! This is Mom! Whatever is going on, she'll kick its ass! You know what, I DID!

It was a long hard process to heal from this. My Guys were right there every step of the way, poking and prodding me to get up and move. Making me look up and see what that might be out there naturally would help my situation. Oh yeah, by the way, they were on me about getting help earlier but this was one of those times that I refused to listen because of the insurance that I didn't have.

Once I started to see a doctor on a regular basis, I was told that if I had waited another forty-eight to seventy-two hours, I wouldn't be here. My body had started to do a complete shutdown. Personally, I think it was my Guys lifting my hand out for my phone to call my friend so that wouldn't happen. Remember, we have the free will. That even goes for living or dying!

Once again, being a person who is always looking for answers, I did my research. There are natural supplements and herbs that can heal the most devastating predicament. Our Earth can help us in ways you could never imagine. Between what the doctors had to offer and what I could do on my side of the equation, slowly but surely, I fought my way back.

It took me a long time to get back to the health that I was. I now have a small heart murmur because of it, but it's a very small price to pay. Through all this, I'm still researching natural ways that not only help me but help others too. There is no medical education in my background, just a need to be able to help when I can.

The point I'm getting at is that my purpose here isn't done yet. I know that from a place deep inside of me. My years of paying attention to nature and all that she has to offer can help anyone that needs it. My craving to find all the answers through research helps this process. All of us are here for a reason, and to be able to use that knowledge for the sake of everyone can be and is very satisfying. No matter how you look at it, we are one. We all count for something! All of us matter, regardless of what numbskull might tell you otherwise.

It saddens me that so many of my friends have passed on without completing their purpose. They had the free will to give up and went to the Other Side. I'd give anything to have Horn Dog in his physical form pushing me and my intelligence to a higher level. But he and others made their choices. It occurs to me that they may have felt that their help would be better from the non-physical side. Horn Dog and a few of my other friends were in the medical field while here in the physical. So, some of the thoughts I have are probably "pushed" through with their help.

Never question why these great thoughts come to you. The willingness to listen and see what the outcome is serves to be more important. We must be the change, myself included. Strive to do what you can. Even the smallest gesture will make a difference in someone's life. Live it and love it!

You can also seek help from everything in nature. For years I have studied relentlessly the powers that Native Americans pursue. They have kept their fingers on the pulse of our true reality and balance that is needed to survive without the modern cures of science. Their collective knowledge is something that goes back thousands of years.

Nature has a way with all her creatures to make it

through parched summers and bitterly cold winters. We're making it harder on them with all that we have done, but they never give up the will to survive!

In my rural area those of us that grew up with the ones that lived in the country learned from a young age how to prepare for whatever is thrown at us. As a matter of fact, I still make my own jams and do my canning every summer with the vegetables that I get. Not just to have food, but to have the homegrown vegetables with all the necessities to keep me healthy. No GMOs for me, thanks!

We are what we eat. As I have to many people before, there is a promise made to my boys that I will live to be 100. Putting vitamins and minerals inside of me can only help make this come true for them. Besides nothing tastes better than a home cooked meal. You can also grow your own vegetables and spices even if you live in an apartment. All you need is sunlight through a window. Seeds can be bought at certain markets or online. All you need is the will to make it so.

Message from my Guys

First, we want to say that you matter. The reason you are in physical form is that it was your wish to be on Earth. From our side, we are trying the best that we can to see that you live the most abundant life.

It is up to you because of your free will to do what is necessary to make your visit on Earth worthwhile. It is all up to you. The vibration of energy that envelops you and is in you seeks to be whole. To do this it is up to you to listen to your own spirit and to those that are here to help you to become all that you should be.

There is a part of you that is trying to come forth and

make the life you have right now the most joyous and happy, and to do this you have to feed the body you are in to be its best. We on the non-physical side continue to show you signs and signals that you can follow. All you must do is listen. Connect to us so we can help. That is why we are here.

Be that shining light that you are supposed to be. Look at what there is to make your physical being the best there is so you can achieve this abundance that is waiting for you. You all have the power to be what you should be. Start this process by nourishing your physical body to work with you on this quest.

Anything and everything that you need to do this is right here waiting for you to take advantage of it. From the vegetables to the herbs. Use that wonderful inner being that you know is there to make this happen.

*When you use a living medicine and get well,
you feel that the world is alive and aware
and wants to help you.
People often talk about saving the Earth,
but how many times have you experienced
the Earth saving you?*

Stephen Buhner

Chapter XI
The Art of Healing Yourself

We that live in the Western world have grown accustomed to running out and grabbing something to eat. Even though it is a quick fill of the stomach, it has damaging effects on your body in the long run.

This will be one of the longest chapters in this book. There are literally years of information accumulation that is going to be shared.

Please don't think that all of this is a quick fix to health. When you do the proper way to enhance your body and mind, it is a slower process. But it's so much more rewarding for you to have the life that you were meant to have.

Often the food that is offered to us is not actually food. It is something that has been concocted through scientists that work for the food industry to make it savory to your taste buds, which makes you want more of it. This makes eating healthy harder to do. It becomes an addiction that is just as bad as cramming drugs down your throat. Don't get me wrong, I love potato chips and cookies! But I try to keep in the back of my mind that moderation is the key.

Anyone that looks can see that our world as we know it is in crisis. We are facing critical times now and what will be happening in the future. At this moment it is the perfect time to usher in a new world in which all of us are full of awareness and live in the world of higher awareness.

If it was up to quite a few of us, the children would be

started at a very young age to be aware of what there is out there for them as far as having the proper nutrition to boost that wonderful brain of theirs and let that education process be a major role in making this happen.

The knowledge of the natural way has definitely gone to the wayside as far as the knowing that for centuries was passed down from ones that were known as healers. Now, it is up to you.

The important thing to remember here is that civilization is just beginning, and the best is yet to come! The great capacity for health and eternal life still lies untapped within us. The key is to be self-sufficient with work, food, and abundance for all.

The following pages will help not only me but others that may be interested. I'm not educated in nutrition or have any degrees, but this is what I've learned through years of researching and taking notes. I'm not responsible for what you decide to do. I urge you to consult with licensed medical professionals and do your own research to find out the best path for you and your health. What follows is merely a sharing of my own accumulated knowledge and personal experience.

The first step is kind of crazy, but it helps more than you know: smaller plates. Yes, I said it, use smaller plates. It's a proven fact that the difference between using a twelve-inch plate versus a ten-inch plate is eating 22% less over the course of a year. This is just a way of tricking the mind that the plate is full.

Also, get rid of the regular table salt. Give Himalayan pink salt a try. It boosts your regular intake of minerals if you use it regularly. Has loads of elements that you need, including potassium (no more muscle cramps) and magnesium. Do your homework and see if this may be a better choice for you.

Now to get down to the nitty gritty of foods and natural herbs that can help you help yourself. Once you start this and keep on track, it gets easier to keep up and you will notice a difference in how you feel. This break down is for symptoms but read through them they may help other things that are going on with you.

Fruits and Vegetables: Eating fruits regularly benefits your body as they are natural sources of vitamins and minerals. This is a great way for you to get the proper functioning of the body.

The nutrients in vegetables are vital for the health and maintenance of your body. Eating a diet rich in fruits and vegetables may reduce the risk of a stroke, heart diseases, cancer, and Type 2 diabetes.

You have probably heard this all before but just keep it as a reminder.

Now let's talk about herbs. These have been my lifesaver. They have played a major role in my getting back on track and living life.

The top silent killer known to us is stress. This can cause your health to decline and creates an opening for many diseases to come through and wreak havoc on your body.

There is a book out there that can help with the education of herbs and spices. The name is *The Clan of the Cave Bear* written by Jean M. Auel.

Here is a list of different herbs that can help relieve the worst and help you keep yourself and your body the best it can be.

Stress

Ginseng: Modulates stress by toning and strengthening your system.

Ashtagandha: This little herb from India gives you endurance. You can mix it with allspice and ginger. It can also help with anxiety over a couple weeks' time.

Holy Basil: This herb has a psychoactive quality, great for relieving stress.

Valerian Root: For the nervous system. Great for insomnia because it relaxes the muscles.

Skullcap: Relieves "monkey mind," which in turn takes away the white noise, relaxes muscles like restless leg syndrome. Teaspoon three times a day.

Kava: Good for restlessness and sleeping problems. This has a lactone base, which is a slight numbing agent.

Blue Vervain: This is for you Type A people. You know who you are, the perfectionist! Helps with feeling overwhelmed.

Lemon Balm: Can make a tea with this one. Great for connecting with your inner self.

Vanilla: Put a teaspoon in your coffee or tea. This can help elevate your mood.

Pain

Feverfew: A real helper for headaches and migraines. Take it on a regular basis for a period of time to get the full benefit.

Turmeric: Anti-inflammatory. Helps support the digestion, especially for the liver and gall bladder. Very medicinal. Personally, I use it as a spice to cook with.

Willow Bark: This is the base for aspirin. Good for pain and fever. Use up to 30 mg to ease pain. Can also bathe in for the body pain. Word of caution, just like aspirin it can thin the blood a little. Made into a tea, two to three cups a day.

California Poppy Root: Great tea at about 30 grams.

Red Pepper: Ground is best. Good for cuts, with this you will heal faster.

Cayenne: Applied as an ointment can help with arthritis. This is another that I use personally. Added as a spice in soups and stews.

Kava: Give a slight sedating effect, good for pain.

Immune System

Astragalus: Nice little herb from China. One of my favorites! Helps the white blood count, which in turn helps tremendously with the immune system. Personally, I take capsules, but it can be put in soup. Several teaspoons daily can help with chemotherapy.

Wild Indigo: Works the same as astragalus.

Mushrooms: Great medicinal tool. Maitake mushrooms can help with cancer. Also helps with longevity.

Reishi: Works with lupus, muscular dystrophy, highly specific. Also helps the autoimmune system.

Auto Immunity

From what I have read this is a body that is out of balance. Much of this problem can be traced back to toxicity of the environment. The first step in helping is to get rid of allergies.

Filtered Water: Having a filter on the tap water is one of the best things you can do to help balance yourself from the harmful additives that is put in our drinking water.

Personally, I have a pitcher next to my kitchen sink that I keep for drinking and making coffee and tea.

Local Honey: One of the best things out there that can help balance what is going on inside of you. Every morning I sweeten my coffee with this miracle medicine. (Bless those little buzzing bees! They are one of the creatures that we really need to make sure stay around. If they go away, so do we!)

Wormwood: This little herb ingested on a regular basis can help balance your system and keep it that way.

Salt: *Real* sea salt, rock salt. I use Himalayan pink salt. This beautiful pink substance is also packed with potassium and magnesium. With the use of this I no longer have any leg cramps. You can also drink saltwater. This can get to the core of the problem.

Throw away that table salt! BLAH! Using sea salt and Himalayan pink can help with asthma, allergies, and autoimmune. This little natural wonder can get to the core of the problem.

In our bodies we have what is called a microbiome. There are approximately three pounds floating around in there! These are on our gut barrier wall and we need them! We as humans have been using fear of bacteria to get rid of these and our guts have become too clean.

So, not having enough microbiome sends messages to our vagus nerve, which is a bunch of sensory nerve cells in our brain controlling our automatic nervous system. There are several bunches of these vagus nerves, but the one that handles the gut is called parasympathetic. This also controls the respiration and the heart rate function, among other things. In turn, these nerves send information from the gut to the brain and vice versa and is linked to stress, anxiety, and fear. This is where we get the saying, "I had a gut feeling." The vagus nerve works like taking a valium naturally.

Because of our extreme cleanliness we need to refuel the microbiome. We have to keep our body in balance for it to work properly.

Maitake or **Shiitake Mushrooms**: These seem to prime the immune system in our gut.

Manuka Honey: This honey is great for using as a probiotic.

Garlic, Onion, Leeks: Having servings of these several times a week in cooking helps the gut biome replenish what has been taken out.

Dandelion: Microbiome enhancer and also good for the liver.

Also eating fruit, chia seeds, and heirloom veggies nourishes our insides and replenishes the microbes.

Healthy Hearts

Did you know that your heart and depression are linked together? Sure, you do! That's why when you suffer from any kind of heartbreak you first feel it in that vital organ and then it goes straight into a state of depression. Loneliness causes more heart problems than needed. By statistics, 75% of people in the USA die of heart attacks!

Through herbs and seasonings, you can help that precious heart of yours.

Hawthorne Tonic: Helps strengthen the heart and reduces inflammation. Lowers blood pressure, which levels the heart rate. Gives proper instruction from the heart to brain (remember the vagus nerve). Best made into a tea.

Red Bark Erginus: Regulates circulation and balances. Helps with rapid heart rate.

Motherwort and **Linden**: Both lower blood pressure and help in menopause.

Hibiscus: Lowers blood pressure and helps with blood circulation and with your diet. Also good for colds.

Garlic and **Onion**: Good for digestion, natural antioxidant. Great for the heart muscle itself! Improves blood flow.

Ashwagandha: Heals all tissues. Gives stamina for the heart.

Sanchi Furikake: Blood tonic for longevity. Builds good blood.

Tan Chi: Helps with blood clotting.

Dunchin: Treats your heart as a whole, helps reduce inflammation. This can also thwart cancer.

Roses: Just the scent relaxes and calms the heart, which includes the muscles. Helps in mending.

Depression

Saffron: Powerful antidepressant. Helps with pain also.

St. John's Wart: Increases production of energy. Interactive with other drugs, so use with caution; this can be too much of a good thing.

Turmeric: Anti-inflammatory in the brain, which in turn helps depression. Personally, I cook with this in my soups and stews. Word of warning: too much will make food bitter.

Rhodiola: Great help with fatigue. Gives strength, so it is also known as "Viking Strength."

Cocoa: Keeps blood sugar balanced. More powerful

when raw. This does not mean you can eat a bunch of chocolate! What it is saying is to use the darker chocolate or find it raw and use in foods.

Raising Energy

Sleep is the most important way to raise your energy. This gives the body and mind rest so it can rejuvenate itself. This will relieve stress and improve your mood. Having the right amount of sleep also can boost your metabolism.

Ashwagandha: This root is best if taken in as a tincture. Regulates the sleep cycle. Helps with food cravings, anxiety, and stress. Makes you *think* better. You can also make a milk with honey and cinnamon.

Valerian: Relaxes nerve system and brings calmness. Take 1 gram the first night, 2 grams for the second night. Lasts about four hours.

Hops: Make into a tea. Helps you go into sleep and stay there.

Skullcap: Quiets the "monkey mind." Can quiet tremors or nervous energy.

Nutmeg: Lowers blood pressure, helps sedate. Can be used for loose stool! Great for the heart. Best if you can find fresh and grind yourself. If found fresh, try to use it within two weeks; after that the potency will diminish. Eat 1 gram at 6 p.m. to be able to sleep by 10 p.m. It takes four hours to kick in.

Lemon Balm: Make into a tea.

Coffee: Use sparingly. It is profound in using as a spark up, then will quit.

Makana: Restores energy.

Roseola: Causes better brain function and restores

energy. Helps in better breathing.

Cancer

This nasty disease hits a personal note with me as you know from the beginning of this book. It is a toxic process where the tumor gets an accumulation of cells and turns them against you. Toxicity is the main culprit.

If you are diagnosed with a cancer, it is always best to rely on doctors that are well trained to help you.

The best way to overcome this monster is to use modern medicine and natural herbs and supplements. Team up and kick its butt.

First, test the vitamins you have in your body. This will require a full blood test. Even though chemo is so hard on one's body, work with herbs to make it better. Conventional and natural therapies should be done *together*.

The main thing to do is to build up the body so the immune system is at its best which in turn will kill off dormant cancer cells.

Vitamin C: Can help with cancer by 45% if in high doses. It also helps with the treatment of chemotherapy.

Medicinal Mushrooms: Maitake and shiitake are good for cooking. Using 3 grams modulates the immune system. Reishi mushrooms are another choice.

Ginger, Ginseng: Will help your immunity to prevent cancer.

Noni Pepper: Is all medicinal.

Turmeric: Antioxidant.

Golden Milk with White Turmeric. Golden milk is a blend of herbs and super foods mixed together to give you the punch you need to boost your immune system to the top.

Blueberries, Ginger, Garlic: All of these will help your body fight away the toxicity and replenish your body from chemotherapy.

Plus, I must mention **Hemp**. Actual THC makes a difference. Hopefully it can be found in a CBD oil.

Hormone Health

Deer Antler Velvet: Stimulates testosterone.

Damiana: Herb from Mexico. Gives you the feel-good emotion.

Frankincense: With cinnamon you can boil and the aromatherapy with induce an enhancing mood.

Ginseng: Libido enhancer.

Ashwagandha: Preservation of calm energy. Gives balance to hormones/testosterone. Helps longevity, muscular strength, and stamina. This is a brain herb.

Saw Palmetto: Contains omega-3 fatty acids and nourishing compounds.

Pine Tree Root: Hormone/testosterone enhancer.

Cocoa: Mood enhancement, raises energy. If made into a salve it will also enhance healing!

Chaste: Hormone balancing herb. Nourishes energy. Finding the berry is the most effective way to use.

Brain Function

If it's good for the heart, it's good for the brain! If you can enhance the quality of what you eat, this will bring the natural nutrients to the brain.

After my ordeal in the hospital and recuperating, the one thing I noticed was my brain just wasn't connecting like it should. This realization came one day when I went to spell "squirrel" and couldn't. All through my life I've been an excellent speller of words. After many years of being behind a desk and compiling documents of all sorts, this was a huge blow to me.

With careful study on the subject and research, like I do, this good old brain of mine is just about back where it should be. There are episodes of remembering past personal memories, but my boys have learned to hit on a few highlights, and this triggers the memory to come back. Once the memory is front and center, it stays with me. Also found that vitamin B12 helps with pumping the brain and getting those cobwebs out.

Enhancing the quality of what you eat brings in the nutrients that are needed for the brain. So here we go!

Canatella: Grown in Oregon, a liquid herbal blend. Calming effects. Can mix with skullcap.

Gotu Kola: Herb from the parsley family. It can do just about everything for the brain. Calms the nervous system. Great for dementia. Cell regenerator. Also great for the complexion and Multiple Sclerosis too! It is considered a "super food." Great for anti-aging and longevity. Make it up like you would do spinach, 30 grams dried or 60-90 grams fresh to get quicker results. (Also great for varicose veins!)

Rosemary: Powerful instigator for recall. Aromatherapy works with this too. Good for dementia. Can be made into a tea or tincture. Great antiseptic.

Sage, Turmeric, Blueberry: Full of amino acids that are needed for a stronger brain.

Walnuts: Great for pushing brain activity and helps develop more than three dozen neurotransmitters to enhance brain functions.

Calemus: Cognition enabler. Great for memory enhancement. Works well with autism.

Bacopa: Works for young and old. Helps ADHD, Alzheimer's, and anxiety. Also has been known to help allergic conditions. Made into a tonic, it helps fight stress.

Gingko: Helps circulation, reduces inflammation, and increases blood flow.

Ashtagandha: Supports coping. Brain and mood neutralizer. Great for stroke recovery and Multiple Sclerosis.

Andrographis: Good for rheumatoid arthritis, Multiple Sclerosis. Helps with the long term.

Huper Zine: Works on Parkinson's, dementia, Multiple Sclerosis. Can give great results.

Lyme Disease

Something that I learned for doing all this research is that Lyme Disease could be contagious! Bell's palsy can be a symptom. Common symptoms are bone and neck pain/tension, achiness. It can also imitate any disease and cause neurological problems like forgetting words, etc.

Raw Probiotics: Good if you have taken antibiotics.

Japanese Knotweed: Blood mover, seeks infection in body. Lowers inflammation.

Astragalus: Great at boosting the immune system.

Cat's Claw: Immune booster. Anti-Inflammatory.

Fur Babies Included

Since putting this together and being the animal lover that I am, I am including a few things you can do for your fur babies. They must have the proper diet just like us.

The worst thing that you can give them is

preservatives, including BHT (butylated hydroxytoluene), BHA (butylated hydroxyanisole), and propylene glycol ethoxyquin. These are carcinogenic, which are bacteria killers. Just like us, pets need good bacteria in their bodies.

Another is fillers, which can be found in the food that we buy at the store. Bad grains, for instance, include barley, white rice, and especially corn and wheat. Absolutely under any circumstances do *not* give them soy! Meat byproducts are not that good for a pet's diet either. Chicken and beef are all byproducts made from bone meal, which doesn't give pets the nutrients they need.

Deli meat is another food that you shouldn't include in their diet because it is extremely high in sodium. Like us, consuming too much is not a good thing.

The best thing for our little family of fur is probiotics that will give them the good bacteria needed for their digestion. That includes pea flour, carrots, flax, ginger, and cherry root.

Super nutrients would include things with doses of B, A, E, and K vitamins and folic acid, phosphorus, iron, copper, magnesium, and iodine.

Organic meats have all the nutrients and carries high doses of vitamin D. Try to feed your furry loved one raw as much as possible. Turkey heart and beef liver is the best. When feeding my fur babies, I try to include a vegetable that I myself have eaten.

The best way to keep them healthy is to keep yourself healthy as well. Here is a list of mutual foods that you can share: peanut butter, chicken, cheese (the real stuff not that stuff that is processed), carrots, yogurt, pumpkin, eggs, green beans, salmon, sweet potatoes, apples, and oatmeal (only the kind you have to cook, not the instant stuff).

There are many recipes out there for your pets that will give them the boost they need to live long lives. I make one for my dogs that when done can be broken up into kibbles and included with their regular dog food.

Message from my Guys

From the beginning of life on Earth, there has been all that you need to live in harmony. Many of the things that you need are right outside your window. With the growth of all and being able to converse with others across the world this has only become easier and better.

Never be afraid of what can be. Look for the will to say what will be. Part of healing is having the state of mind that nothing can stop you from being and doing. Once again it is part of your free will. We ask from this side in the non-physical, why would you not try to be more of what you are? Tap into the energy that is all around you to take advantage of. Be that living, breathing, beautiful, physical spirit.

Life is such a precious thing. From the moment it takes its first breath until the moment it exhales its last. You are not there in the physical to just pass day by day and not achieve some sort of your own greatness. Everyone—and we mean everyone—is there on Earth to make some kind of difference. To work together and become all that there is. To see each day as a new beginning to start something that can benefit yourselves and others.

This is why we have pushed Tinker to show you all the aspects of what you can do to connect and be with your own spirits of the non-physical. All of this so far in this book is showing you different ways to do just that. Like it has been said previously, it is all a balance and flow. It isn't a hard thing to do. All that is required is to be aware and find that balance. Once this is found, all that is left is to ride the wave of energy and enjoy every moment.

Each of you have your own unique being with the same goal as each other of being all that you can. Just keep in mind and in soul that with a little knowledge you can go so far. Farther than you could ever imagine. With the knowledge of being the best you can be at any given time brings in a knowing of a bigger and better way. It can only grow more and more. You can make this possible; all you have to do is give it a try and keep pushing. Don't give up! If there is a setback, take a deep breath and try again. You will get there.

In the following pages we have asked Tinker to enlighten you what mostly is out there for you to be able to connect with us. Us meaning your own Guys, as Tinker puts it.

The first part is the balance of you yourself. These pages from here on give existence in a way to know yourself spiritually and find that unique connection that you should have to converse with the non-physical.

This is something that is not just for certain ones. This is something that you *all* can do. We want you to connect with us. To be able to find the personal answers that are you and just for you to find. There is a great number of us in the non-physical that are knowledgeable in all aspects of life. Many of us can help with any and all things.

It is fine to look for guidance along the way, but there comes a point in your physical life that you should be able to have your own personal guidance that can enlighten you and awaken all that is available to you.

We are here waiting for you! Please know that we have been patient and will continue to be. From the non-physical side, you are our light! We want to shine with you. We want to work with you to be that rainbow of all that there is. Keep looking for us, we are here! We are here and ready to make everything that you want to be possible.

We are the ones that you feel as you hesitate, that have those hands at your back pushing you forward. It is us that whisper in your ear that this is the right decision that you are making. Feel us, listen for us. Flow with us!

*Your journey
may be long...
But with Angels
by your side,
you'll never
be alone.*

*Melanie Beckler
www.AskAngels.com*

Chapter XII
Signs, Signs Everywhere a Sign

They're out there. Signals and signs from those that are now part of the Divine. Being of a different frequency than us in the physical, we need to increase our awareness for the moment and start noticing the guidance that they are trying to give us.

This guidance comes in all forms of messages, dreams, and direct insight. As you can tell from this book, mine comes from many directions. They have a way of throwing something in your direction, like a clue or a hint, which can serve to nudge you in the right direction.

When you become aware and focus on the acknowledgement and appreciate what they are trying to do, they will often increase the frequency. These signs or signals can come in a variety of ways depending on your current status of challenges, next steps you may want to take, or you may just have a question that you need answered, you know, like a nudge in the right direction.

When you notice a sign from your Angels, breathe, be aware, and once again give them a thanks for reaching out. As you do this more often and practice your present moment of awareness there will be an acknowledgement of more in tune and sync with your own personal Guys. Here are some of the more noticeable signs or signals that can show up when you least expect them.

Feathers: This is one that is a frequent and commonly used sign that they are close. Personally, my Guys know that I have a knowledge of what kind of feather is being presented to me, so I also take in consideration what that kind of feathered friend is being represented. What I mean by this is, if a feather is found, say it belongs to a raven, I know that ravens represent a way of passing to the Other Side. They are considered in many beliefs to be a spiritual being that can relay messages or be guided to you from beyond the veil. At that moment, I take in consideration of what is needed in my life with the closeness of being in touch. Each feather to me represents the meaning of the bird. Mockingbirds are go-getters and have a beautiful song along the way. If you have a question and receive a feather, take the extra step and see what the spiritual meaning is for that bird. You can always use Google to see what kind of feather you have received. Become aware of the different birds in your area and their colors. This will help you find out the particular feather you have in your grasp.

Clouds: With clouds it is usually a shape or color. Once, while I was in a deep mood of thought—you know, that kind of ho hum we go through from time to time—I stopped at a traffic light, looked up and there was the most beautiful cloud full of the colors of a rainbow, but it shimmered and had a sparkle to it. This told me that I needed to lighten up and know that things are going to get better.

Music: Angels can get a message across so quickly with music, especially if you know the words and are in tune with what they are trying to say. There are messages in the lyrics on the radio or even in your head. My Guys seem to come through a lot when music is involved.

Here's a good one. When I started to write this book,

my thought was, "What is my title going to be?" This thought stayed in my head for a few days when out of the blue my Guys told me to turn on the radio. Well, there was the name of my book, loud and clear. Started singing along, and it hit me! So now you know how the name was discovered.

Coins: Finding coins or any currency in general is a common sign of support and guidance from your Guys. If you find one in your path, pay attention! Does the date on the coin hold any meaning for you? Was there a question of financial help that you had been contemplating? Would the date ring a bell about something that may have happened at that moment in time? What was your thought right before you found the coin? This could be a sign or a symbol that you are supported. Whether or not the penny is heads up doesn't matter, and I pick it up and immediately look at the date. No bad luck for me, just a message that is trying to come through.

Sparkles of Light: Those that have passed to the non-physical become beings of love and light. Unexplained lights of shimmering or flashes of color are very common ways of experiencing your Guys. Sometimes a streak of light can catch your attention without actually having a light source, or a bright star catches your eye. Light flashing off an object in an unusual way or an orb of light hovering nearby are signs of your Guys coming through. Here's a test: close your eyes and if you still see the light, it's more than likely that they are with you. This is the time that you can relax, take a deep breath and if you're ready, your Guys may expand the light before you or envelope you into their angelic glow to bring you uplifting feelings, healing, or rejuvenation.

Rainbows: Rainbows are one of the most common symbols of love of the Divine. If you have asked for assistance from your Guys and shortly after see a rainbow, know that your thoughts have been heard and they are trying their best to assist you. This is just a confirmation that they are there. A rainbow orb around our moon, a double rainbow, or a rainbow appearing when it hasn't even rained are extra splendid signs from your Guys, and they are bringing you definite validation and encouragement from above.

Temperature Change: Sometimes when one of your Guys enters and makes a presence in our physical world, you can experience a change of temperature, which in turn is a great validation that they are with you. You may feel a sudden warm glowing light around you. Or the opposite can happen, a chill or cold feeling that usually comes with a tingling or pressure in your head or neck, like feeling your hair stand up a little. It shouldn't be an uncomfortable experience but a sense of excitement that is a physical manifestation from your Guys!

A Sense of Feeling: If you feel a presence near, they probably are! This is the feeling I get when Horn Dog is close. That feeling of someone present or who has just walked past you when no one is there. That feeling that someone is in the room, but you know it is empty. They may reach out to you with a very subtle nudge and be close to you. This is usually a time when you can feel their love. They can brush your arm or rest their hand on your shoulder. There will be times when the sense of that unconditional love overwhelms you. This is a sure sign that they are there.

There could be times of a chill in the air close to you

and all of a sudden an object will appear in your eyes that you hadn't noticed. Pay attention, your Guys are there with you. Maybe take a look at the object and see if it can help you.

Voices: Hearing the guiding voice of your Guys is one of the most beautiful things that can happen! My Guys are always whispering in my ear and giving me guidance. Yes, it is usually a whisper. Sometimes it is so soft I have to ask them to repeat and speak a little louder. Don't ever assume that you are making this up! Hearing the guidance of your Guys is the greatest form of reassurance and comfort that you are never alone.

Numbers: This is a big one! There are all kinds of ways that through numbers, your Guys can get a message across. Have you ever noticed that you may be seeing a number repeatedly and you can't explain why? Well, start noticing and see what the message is that they are trying to give you. All repeated numbers have a specific meaning. Listed below are some of the master Divine numbers that they can use. There are numerous books that can give you numbers from one to 999, or just Google the meaning!

111: Intuition. Encourages you to keep following your spirit. You're on the right path if you see this. Listen to your gut and heart.

222: Right One. Right place, right time. Trust in what you want and don't think of things you don't want when you see this number.

333: Equilibrium. Mind, body, and spirit. Focus on all three aspects. Don't neglect one for another when you see this number.

444: Protection. The universe and your spiritual Guys are protecting you. Pay attention to your thoughts and your environment when you see this number.

555: Change. A change is occurring, and the universe is moving things around for you when you see this number.

666: Step Back. Take a step back to rethink and ask yourself if what you are doing is right or wrong. (No, this isn't a bad number, it's just that simple minds have made it seem that way.)

777: Inner Strength. Release all fear and be strong at heart. Look forward to the future with excitement when you see this number.

888: Balance. You're in harmony with the universe and your thoughts and actions are also in harmony when you see this number.

999: Wrap Up. Time to start a new journey, so wrap up the loose ends, and let go of what doesn't serve you. Prepare for the next level when you see this number.

Advertisements: You may have asked for guidance and all the sudden the billboards or signs seem to jump out at you with what they say. Stay open and alert because you may notice a certain word or phrase on several street names, shop signs, or billboards. This is an indication to follow and see what may be in store for you. There may be a wonderful experience waiting just beyond the horizon!

Try to remember that life is a growing process. We grow through the knowledge of what is going on around us and the awareness of our Guys trying to help. No matter what the process is, try to give recognition and grow through giving. Your success in doing this is that you earn more splendor in your consciousness. This is the key: think of yourself as a channel through which creative activities flow and there will be no limit to what is coming.

Position yourself squarely on the side of abundance and prosperity and just let something good happen. With signs coming in from those that love you on the Other Side of the veil, this is the starting point of changing your life and the realization that you can change by altering your thoughts to include those in the non-physical.

The starting point to changing your life to experience abundance is the realization that you can alter your own thoughts. Once you start taking responsibility for your own life and letting those around you in the non-physical take part in this endeavor, the truth of being in balance and accomplishing is what meant for you will become clearer.

Be present and in the now. Be aware and look for signs that your Guys are trying to give you. They always have a way of letting their presence be known. Try to tune in and experience what they have to offer.

There will be times of failure. Try to remember that nothing is ever a complete loss. You are an individualized expression of creative flow. No one is as unique as you. There is always an answer for every problem. Let your Guys flow through and help.

Message from my Guys

We know that watching all that is happening around you can be both pleasant and a burden. What really counts is what is happening *within* you. There is limitless potential of creative substance and each present experience can be one of the greatest opportunities for you to go through. You are a part of the substance of infinity as much as we are.

There will come a time that you can look back and

realize that what may have happened and was considered at the time a failure is now the best possible thing that could have happened. Once you have become aware of your own Guys being there and helping, you will find that the failures that you have experienced in the past become fewer and farther between. In your mind, you will start to see and hear the voice of reason. That is us helping you. We try to let you know that that there are all kinds of limitless possibilities and opportunities, which will in turn give you new ideas, new strengths, and some of the greatest visions possible.

Something wonderful is always just around the corner. We are here to help extend your horizons. Signs are abundant for you to follow. Become aware of your feelings and know that this is one of the keys to completing what you are intended to accomplish.

Be Silent...
Focus...
Listen to Spirit.
You will be guided
every time!

One Who Gathers Tribes

Chapter XIII
More Than Just Creatures

If there is a civilization out there amongst the stars and they are observing us and our planet, there is no doubt that among the millions of species on Earth, we homo sapiens stand out. We sit on top of the food chain, our habitats are all over the entire planet, and in recent times there has been an explosion of technology, social activities, and artistic advancements.

How remarkable it is to sit back and observe how far we have come in a short amount of time. But you must wonder how we as a species got so far. Almost 100% of all the species that have ever lived on Earth are now extinct. Not only have we made it through and survived, but we have seen intellectual and technological progress beyond any other life form.

The fact that we as humans can read and write articles and contemplate the adversity of our nature and mental abilities is awe inspiring.

With our brains—a mere three pounds of mass—we can contemplate ourselves and the meaning of infinity. Self-reflective consciousness boosts our abilities for self-identification, recognition, and monitoring.

But there is one thing that you must keep in that wonderful mind: everything in our world as we know it is made up of clumps of matter, stardust that originated in the challenge of the stars.

We and everything around us are not only the universe, but the universe is also within us. Some of us possess a higher consciousness than others. The ultimate equation for this is how we ask ourselves the ultimate questions and put that forth to the masses. If we can understand the meaning of other species that live among us, then we have a head start.

In recent times, we as humans have gotten away from looking beyond what we can't see right in front of us. The other species that live with us still have the capability of naturally knowing everything just by using the vibrations and energy that our Earth provides. They are linked with us also and if you take the time to start paying attention to what they do, your life can have a huge change for the good.

Indigenous peoples still have that connection. They pay attention to the world and its inhabitants closely. They realize that each one of us has a spirit animal that helps guide and protect us on our journey and usually the characteristics coincide with our own. Even science gives us evidence that DNA matches are found between us and many other animals, even plants. This means that without a doubt all living things on this Earth are infinitely intertwined.

Native Americans refer to all living things as people. Because of this belief there is an intricate connection, so if your soul sends out an SOS, all other living things hear the signal. This is part of the Universal Mind. So, when you need help or guidance, all the living things hear your heart and the appropriate soul appears, whether it's animal or plant! Many times, these are known as our spirit animal guides or totem animals.

To find out what your spirit animal is, make yourself aware of a few basic steps. Here are a few things to look out for.

Pay Attention: Start noticing all that keep appearing to you. Whether it is outside, a song you hear, movie, books, conversations. If a certain animal keeps appearing, they are trying to help you in some way.

There was a friend of mine that just couldn't seem to locate her spirit animal. But I had noticed in our conversations that she was seeing a spider outside her bedroom window. Then when she was out to do some camping in the woods, she made a comment that as she parked her vehicle, a spider came down out of a tree and hung in front of her right outside her windshield. My comment was "So you can't seem to find your spirit animal even when it sits right in front of you staring you in the face!"

She was looking for a furry friend, but as you will find out on your quest to locate yours, they find and appear to you not the other way around. My message to her was this: if you look at the characteristics of a spider, it is a pillar of strength and cares for the family around it. I reminded her that all her life she has taken care of others, even children that weren't her own. *She* is the one that people turn to for guidance.

Meditation and journeying: This will usually involve being able to attain an altered state of consciousness and the use of deep imagery or visualization with the specific intention of meeting your spirit animal guide or guides.

Dreams: You see animals. We as humans often don't believe that we can receive messages from our spirit animal guides, so they may appear to us in our dream state. Many times, it is easier for us to trust our dreams rather than our own intuition during our hours of awake time.

Native Americans call all the beings power animals. In their traditions, the medicine men and women work closely with spirit animals and refer to them more commonly as animal totems. Power animals and animal totems are both considered to reside in the spirit guide realm.

Our spirit animal guides can be grouped by their natural habitats. The whale, octopus, and shark are water animals. Elephants, pandas, and cats are land animals. All birds—whether they fly or not—are our avian guides. Reptilian and insect animal guides are self-explanatory. Reptilians along with insects are found in different places all over the world. It depends on which you connect with as to what their natural habitat is. But each group are themed to their healing and knowledge.

Land animals: Relate to the physical world and grounding.

Birds: Show strength, freedom, and desire.

Water Animals: Show spirituality and spiritual development.

Reptiles: Relate to the inner self and outer self.

Insects: Relate to persistence and determination.

Each and every one of our animal guides has a spiritual role to play. They appear to us for many different reasons, but they usually have a reason that can be grouped into lifelong guides, messengers, tests, and journeys.

Lifelong: Lifelong guides are with you for your lifetime and reflect you. This may be determined by your spiritual path and what you are like as a person.

Messengers: These messenger animal guides come to you with a warning, message, or some sort of knowledge to impart and will stay with you until their job is complete.

Tests: Animal spirit guides can appear to test you, and these are sometimes known as "Shadow Spirits" that show you when they appear in your life. Can make you feel nervous, anxious, and very apprehensive at the start, but by the time they pull away in your journey, you will understand more about your limits and the energy of that animal.

Journeys: Our journey with the animal spirit guides depends on what direction we are headed on our path. This also has a lot to do with our journey in life. There may be a specific occasion that can arise, tasks that need to be completed or certain phases we go through in life. This is when a specific animal will come forward and they will help you through this.

When working with your totem animal, you need to keep in mind the nature of that creature. Are they the ultimate survivalist, predators, or are they social creatures or loners? Do they have physical power, or are they gentle? Are they scavengers or hunters?

All of this will help you understand why they appear in your life and maybe even guide you when you are trying to determine your own spirituality and the path you may be walking at that time in your life.

Personally, for years my totem (or spirit) animal was the red-tailed hawk, a powerful hunter. They are one of the messengers of the spirit world, which in turn meant there were powerful lessons that I needed to learn to expand my knowledge and vision.

Later in life I noticed a change in my totem animal. No longer was there the presence of my hawk when I went out, but there seemed to be a raven wherever I went. They would call out to me. Seemed that they needed my attention whenever possible. They let me know that they were always there; one particular bird would always be in my large elm tree in my front yard. As time went by, he found a mate and now there are several living close to me. Keeping contact with them made me notice their habits and from a short distance I witnessed them teaching their young to fly and soar through the skies above me.

The raven is the reflection of the universe and its mystical ways. I now have a strong and mysterious force surrounding me. Their beautiful black feathers that with the light of the sun gleams the colors of the rainbow show that they are messengers between heaven and Earth. They are magicians showing rebirth and renewal. I finally realized that my awareness had taken place.

Now any time that I'm out and about, there is always a raven there with me. They are known to me as my brothers. When I see one, I always acknowledge its presence by saying "I see you, my brother!" with a nod and a smile. They call back to me, letting all know that I am taken care of.

Keep in mind that when you are seeking an animal guide, you don't get to choose what it will be. It could be anything from a bumble bee to a grizzly bear. They may stay with you for life, or they may leave once they have completed their tasks in helping you complete yours.

Wherever the animal takes you please remember to be open to its message, its voice, and its energy. While it would be cool to have a majestic leopard as your own personal guide, keep in mind that it may not turn out that way.

Once you start noticing all creatures in nature, you will find that others beside your totem animal will appear when you need help. They are so in touch with energy and vibration that they seem to know when to show up.

To be able to tell when they are there to help you, they make sure that you notice them. Most of the time, for me, they will make eye contact. So, you might have to look away from your smartphone now and then to get the help that is offered to you!

There have been times when I've stepped outside to do something in the yard and notice that I'm being watched. Once when out trimming in the back yard I looked up and a huge turkey was standing there looking back at me. I live in a small area with yards that are about an acre. It is quite unusual to see a turkey. We both just stood there looking at each other, and then he turned and walked away.

Once the yard work was finished, I immediately went in and looked up what it meant spiritually to see a turkey. The meaning is the turkey spirit is closely associated with the abundance of Earth. It symbolizes all the blessings you receive from Mother Nature. When the turkey comes into your life, it is to remind you to honor what the Earth has to offer. More importantly, be ready to share your gifts, talents, and blessings with the world. So here I am doing exactly that.

There is a book called *Animal Spirit Guides* by Steven D. Farmer. It is a great read for those seeking to find out what all the different animals mean. Also included is how to call on some of Earth's creatures for guidance. If you need help with a problem and you seek an answer or may need guidance in getting something solved, this book is wonderful.

For a quick reference, you can always Google what information you may be looking for. There are many of those that have been a part of the studies of everything there is to know on animal spirit guides and totems. They have spent their lives looking and studying the characteristics of each and every possibility that is with each creature on our beautiful Earth.

Many Native Americans have put what they know into writing and decided to share their wealth of information. They see the new coming and want to be there for everyone and everything involved.

*Crystals are
living beings in
the beginning of
creation.*

Nikola Tesla

Chapter XIV
Being a Legal Stoner

The magic of stones! It is something that can push manifestation to its limits. Having the love of crystals and all they have to offer us, beautiful stones have been around since the beginning of time. They have played a part in our lives since the first man came into being.

Many studies have been conducted through the years and it is a fact that crystals emit vibrations that can affect our minds and bodies, and some stones can conduct energy. It was discovered in 1880 if you put pressure on various crystals—including quartz, topaz, and tourmaline—electricity is created. Because of this discovery, crystals are now used as elements in computers, TV screens, iPhones, and satellites. It's also been discovered that crystals can increase the alkalinity of water.

There have been so many things that have been discovered with the use of crystals, even the benefit of using them in skin care and massage therapy for energizing your body.

The power of crystals will help you better connect with your own personal intuition and give you the ability to hear those subtle messages from the universe. The great thing about crystals is you can practice with any stone that you are drawn to. Since crystals are a natural amplifier of energy, they can deepen your meditation and grant you access to spaces you may not have discovered on your own.

Each stone has its own vibration. Here are some examples of how you can use crystals.

Apophyllite: Using this on your third eye will magnify the power of your psychic vision and if you work with it closely you will experience a mild vibration.

Azurite: Known for its ability to clear the mind, can also help access your inner wisdom. Expands your mind so you can focus and zero in on what may be important. With a busy mind it's hard to think straight, so use this stone to get focused. A great stone for using in a water elixir.

Celestite: Helps smooth the transition into a peaceful state of awareness. There are healers that believe it helps them tap into their psychic and intuitive abilities. Working with this stone during meditation can encourage the art of downloading messages from the spiritual realm and receiving guidance and inspiration.

Lepidolite: Natural anxiety reliever, soothes your thoughts and brings calm to your mind. Great for meditating when you feel anxious, worried, or stressed. Brings ease to chaotic or overwhelming thoughts and guides you back to your natural state of being.

Pietersite: An excellent stone for working in the Akashic Records.

Howlite: Helps in connecting with your past lives.

Malachite: Helps align and harmonize the physical, emotional, mental, and spiritual levels of your being. For those that strive too hard trying to control their reality. Great for grounding, but do *not* take internally!

Serpentine: Gives peace of mind and puts you into gentle connection with Angels. Also good for enhancing your meditation.

Many people I know use crystals in their drinking water or elixir. Water is a living liquid vibration. Crystals purify and cleanse the water, which makes this a partnership and a great union in healing. Here is a list of stones you can use with or without water.

Abalone Shell: Treats excessive anxiety and fear for others. Helps psychic connection with water.

Amazonite: Helps treat feelings of social inadequacy.

Amber: For despair. It also helps to balance your mind and feelings and gives psychic protection. Gives the sense of health and healing.

Aquamarine: Brings calm to tenseness, stress, and strain. Has a quiet clarity to an overactive mental body. Increases your ability to achieve a neutral serene state of mind.

Amethyst: Helps in opening the third eye, which in turn helps to better perceive the unseen around you. Raises vibration to a more spiritual level. Can also give you the freedom to make your own decision and plans. Great stone for using in a water elixir.

Aragonite: Helps in overcoming the feeling of helplessness. Acts as a stabilizing stone. Helpful for those who have a focus for solely needing a spiritual pursuit.

Aventurine: Strengthens and stabilizes us during our growth experiences. Helps with moving into and through new experiences with stamina, grace, and perseverance. Good for pioneers and trailblazers in spirituality because of its gift of pride, aloofness, mental rigidity, and high mindedness.

Beryl: Promotes patience, perseverance, discipline, and open heartedness. Worshipped by the ancient Hebrews. Helps with low self-esteem.

Black Tourmaline: Great stone for restlessness because it can exchange old unwanted energies for fresh, clean, natural energy. Can be used as a precision tool for releasing of toxic energy from the mind, emotions, and especially the physical body. Offers protection and grounding.

Bloodstone: Strengthens the connection we need to Earth. Brings in a stronger flow of earth energies. Helps with stability after a trauma or emotional upset. For people that demand unquestioning affection.

Black Onyx: Can be used for frustration with the slow development of events. Also, for those of us that are unable to confront our emotions.

Blue Lace Agate: Good for communication, especially for those who have difficulty in being heard by others or need confidence in sharing their truth. Gives clarity of thought and unwavering intent regarding what matters most to you.

Calcite: For people that have the fear of not formulating fresh goals. Helps with feeling of emotional confinement.

Carnelian: Allows a greater flow of energy to the meridians. Increases the etheric body's ability to access spiritual energy. Helps energize and clear the energetic interface with the body.

Chrysocolla: Great for those of us that are stuck in an over-organized life routine. It will open, soften, and expand the inner dimension of the heart. Helps release tension and armoring against giving and receiving love.

Chrysoprase: Treats arrogance and egotism because it brings the heart into harmonious union with the green energy of Earth. Synchronizes the subtle bodies with the heart energy of the planet.

Citrine: Amplifies qualities of concentration, centering and using the rational mind. Harmonizes the mental with higher spiritual laws, increases access to Divine truth and intelligence.

Diamond: Strengthens our ability to act in alignment with a Divine purpose. Harmonizes personal will and helps activate that will to its highest form.

Dioptase: For the ones that deny themselves emotionally. Excellent for furthering spiritual attunement.

Dolomite: Encourages charitable actions, giving, and generosity. Also great for those of us that fear failure or lack resources.

Emerald: Energizes the Divine feminine. Gives balance and cleansing to the heart. Gently coaxes the heart to allow a greater experience of love in the physical body.

Fluorite: Brings increased energy to the physical body by breaking up blockages in the etheric body.

Gold: Brings in and enables us to access physical reality in the highest aspects of our own personal identity. Helps tap into our inner truth, joy, and wisdom as a source of creative power.

Green Jasper: Reconnects our body with the earthly rhythms when there has been a disruption to the natural flow. Restores earthly sensuality.

Green Tourmaline: For those that have idealistic goals but experience disappointment.

Hematite: Strengthens energetic boundaries for those that feel defenselessness. Promotes emotional independence rather than codependency. Helps to maintain a state of compassionate detachment while witnessing an intense emotional experience in another. Helps contain emotional experiences in a responsible way.

Herkimer Diamond: Highly developed transmitter of white light. These have an extremely high vibration and harmonious energy. Promotes clarity of vision and stimulates healing at all levels. Facilitates clarity during the dream state. For those of us with the inability to achieve goals. A wonderful receiver of conditional love. Also known to enhance clairvoyant abilities.

Jade: Helps in being realistic about ideals. Aids in the practical mystic vibrations of peace, balance, and timeless simplicity. Great for staying centered in the moment with awareness and acceptance of your true essence.

Kunzite: Opens the heart to the awareness of our angelic presence. Can help us to experience the spiritual love of the kingdom of Angels and integrate it into our physical bodies.

Labradorite: Relieves tension arising from frustration. Bathes and nourishes the entire energy system with full spectrum of light. Renews and refreshes our perspective. Helps us to see the magnificent in the mundane and connect to the Divine in the ordinary. Deepens meditation and raises consciousness. Stimulates inner awareness, bringing you closer to discovering your true self. Helps to unfurl your true life purpose and uncover your destiny.

Lapis Lazuli: Helps enhance awareness, insight, and truth. A healing stone that was used by pharaohs. Can deepen meditation by amplifying the ability to hear information from physical and non-physical sources. Clears confusion between hearing and knowing.

Magnesite: For those that experience emotional insecurity. Helps with disappointment and unfulfilled hopes.

Moldavite: An energetic window into universal perspective and connectedness. Helps to stay in the present moment while accessing what we need to express our earthly potential.

Moonstone: For those that feel threatened by their environment. Also great for those that are reckless in spending money. Cleanses and circulates energy in the emotional body. Increases intuition in both men and women.

Moss Agate: Healing stone for harmony and repressed sexual feelings. Good stone for wealth and growing new crops.

Nephrite: Releases the feeling of overwhelming details. For those that have the emotion of being pulled in many directions at once.

Opal: Feeds the body with the full spectrum of luminous colors of the ether. Rejuvenates your old emotions and enables you to build mental forces so in turn this can give you the ability to rebuild the depletion of the color frequencies in the aura. Replenishes creative energies. Good for suppressed agitation from resistance and forming stimulation.

Orange Calcite: Uplifting and warming. Dispels darkness and grief. Amplifies the body's ability to assimilate light at a cellular level.

Pearl: Helps with emotional excitement associated with fear. Promotes the release of layers of irritation in the mental and emotional bodies that are seen in the physical as hardness and inflexibility. Will turn antagonism for yourself or your illness into awareness and acceptance.

Pink Tourmaline: Helps with surfacing old emotional patterns and resolving them. For lack of creativity through repressed personality.

Peridot: The stone of new beginnings. Helps stabilize the subtle bodies during the incubation period of new ideas and creative projects. Initiates new cycles of learning and experience.

Pyrite: Helps build up the energetic foundation in life based on your highest personal truth. Strengthens your sense of self about group dynamics and peer pressure. Lets you see the honor in your values.

Quartz: Protests against adverse environmental influences. Amplifies intentions while clearing, cleansing, and healing.

Rose Quartz: Promotes love and inner peace. Opens and softens the heart. Helps you connect to and nurture your inner child. Harmonizes the heart by forcing you to maintain intimacy with yourself and others.

Rutilated Quartz: Promotes precise alignment with higher sources of energy and inspiration which in turn helps us physically anchor our abilities to access, synthesize, and communicate information from other dimensions. For those of us that overemphasize sensuous luxury.

Shungite: Great for cleaning water that you drink from your tap. It can remove impurities from additives.

Smoky Quartz: Most efficient and powerful for grounding and calming. Provides one of the finest healing tools available. Helps heal fear of emotional interaction with others. Synchronizes the body energy with earth energy. Can regulate and stabilize detoxification of unwanted energies in the physical, mental, and emotional.

Rhodochrosite: Relieves exhaustion arising from frustration. Increases energy, balance, and stability needed in the heart and physical body. Brings a balance of nurturing from Earth energy to the heart with healing.

Rhodolite Garnet: Increases the ability to inhabit the physical body. Reconnects energetically with parts of the body that have been injured or traumatized. Rebuilds the intricate etheric energy in areas that have been disrupted by surgery.

Rhodonite: For those of us that fear criticism and feel physical exhaustion. Strengthens physical and spiritual vitality.

Ruby: Grounds spiritual energy, not physical. Can awaken higher impersonal love. Represents a crystalized version of Divine love.

Sapphire: Gives devotion to Divine purpose. Synchronizes your energy system with your higher purpose. Intensifies the qualities of responsibility and loyalty to your true work on Earth.

Star Sapphire: Promotes trust in the universe. Helps with focusing awareness on what is necessary for the soul's progression in life. Supports energetic connections that help realize your life goals.

Sugilite: Brings physical richness and depth to your spiritual life. Helps with the physicality to manifest a warmer more feminine quality of your spirit. Promotes an easy acceptance of hard striving in the spiritual realm.

Selenite: For those that can't relinquish the past with guilt and have over-active imaginations. Helps to pull back from fantasy worlds.

Sodalite: Gives a sense of calm to weather the storm. Helps in overcoming the desire for inappropriate action during rage and a need for negative attention. Place this stone on the back of the neck to help with headache. Also good for keeping bad vibrations out of your home. Sodalite is above my entry doorway so any bad energy or vibration is checked and stopped at the door and whoever tried to bring it in can take it with them when they leave.

There are many more stones that can be used for cleansing. *Word of warning!* Not all crystals can be used in water. Some have elements that you should not ingest. Do your homework and make sure that your stone is safe to use as a purifier and cleanser for water.

Healing crystals are used in many varieties of illness. Because crystals transmit a frequency, they can alleviate nasty vibrations of unease and discomfort we encounter. It may be no surprise that crystals hold a vibration, both one of their own and of those they work with.

If you want to work with stones intentionally, it is always a good thing to make a grid. Grids are one of the best ways to send out your message to the universe. To start a grid, you will need crystal points, four for each side of the grid. Interline with stones that will help with what you are seeking. Usually it's green for money, pink for love, and so on. Just jump on Google and put in the color of stone for the intent you want.

If it is something that you want to bring into your life, place the points going clockwise. With an intent to go out into the universe, place the points counterclockwise. For example, I have a grid set up and change out the stones I have researched to give or receive my intent. Look on YouTube for different ways you can set up your personal grid.

*You know how every once in
a while you do something and
the little voice inside says,
"There. That's it.
That's why you're here."
And you get a warm glow in
your heart because you
know it's true!
Do more of that.*

Enlightened Consciousness

Chapter XV
Our Children, Our Future

Through the years there have been many studies about change that is happening with humanity. It seems to have started being observed with the flux of what were called hippies. We stayed young looking and believed in peace on Earth.

These were the children born after World War II. They seemed to have a whole different outlook on what the world should be like. I am one of them; we had a strong calling to make the world a better place with a better way of doing things. We didn't (and don't) like to be controlled by authority figures.

Being those with strong will but very sensitive, there was a feeling of being different and that we were definitely here for a reason but—like at the beginning of reading a book—we didn't quite know why.

There was a need in us to stand up for what we believed in. It should be a fair and just world. Life should have meaning instead of just making money.

With each generation after us, there has been an influx of children born with a purpose of making change for good. Each generation has its own collective personality and definitely moves the evolution of humanity in a different direction.

This chapter is a list of the different types of children born after the so-called hippies. It will only touch on the attributes of each generation, but if you feel like you may be one of these, you can dig deeper and research all the studies that have been done. To start there are five generations of Indigo children. Intermingled among them are Crystals, Rainbows, Diamonds, and Starseeds.

Indigo Children: There are several generations of these children. It began with the **Alphas**, born from the 1950s to late 60s. The previous paragraphs explain their generational personality.

Beta Indigo Children: Born from the late 60s to the late 70s. With the Alphas, these children actually have a "youth" gene where they look younger than they actually are. With high IQs, they are self-confident and have an acute intuition. Extremely creative. There may have been suffering of early depression with feelings of helplessness. They maintain strong empathy, and they can't stand stupidity. Betas have a need to explore their sexuality. At times there is low self-esteem, scattered energy, and psychic experience. They may have had UFO encounters.

Gamma Indigo Children: Born from the late 70s to late 80s, the first generation to experience ADHD and ADD, which society explains as aggressiveness, acting out, or fragile introversion. This is the first generation that intermixed the birth of Crystal children. There may be a history of depression or even suicidal thoughts or attempts. Gammas bore easily and are prone to insomnia, restless sleep, and nightmares.

Delta Indigo Children: Born between late 80s and late 90s, known as "pure" ones because they share Crystal children and ADD/ADHD with Gammas. Because of their pureness, they need to be grounded. Because of this there may be a need to get into drugs for the stimulation, but this only makes things worse. Deltas find that warm and deep colors in their environment with slow rhythms help sooth them.

Omega Indigo Children: Born from the late 90s to the late 2000s, the final generation of "pure" ones (Crystal children). This generation will face problems similar to the Deltas, getting accustomed to maneuvering the environment. This generation is generally born in homes of earlier Indigos. Omegas will witness a decline in the population of people from earlier Indigos and may suffer from skin problems and allergies due to high environmental pollution. With this generation is an influx of autistics and those suffering from Asperger's.

For each of the Indigos, the process of awakening usually begins around the age of twenty-eight or twenty-nine and will take about seven and a half years to get through. With all of the Indigos, this is a difficult and dark time. It is the realization of your purpose in life.

With each generation, there is a mature age between thirty-seven and thirty-nine when they will see a recovery of their psychic ability. This gives them all the time to learn to trust their psychic powers and begin their communication with the spirit world. To be able to read thoughts, feelings, and the intentions of others. Those at this age understand the parallel levels of reality and have true insight into the nature of time.

Star Children or **Starseeds**: These individuals were born at different times. They are people who originated as extraterrestrial life from other planets and came to Earth either by birth or as walk-ins. They feel loneliness and isolation, as though they never quite fit in with everyone. Star children were assigned here to help assist Earth and humanity with the ascension process. This is the process of raising energy to a higher vibrational frequency and involves a shift from the denser and ego-centric state of duality consciousness to a more unified and heart-based consciousness. They may catch themselves looking at the stars, and there is some particular point out there that draws their interest without knowing why. Sometimes they pick up a frequency from someone (a fellow Star child) that they don't from others. All their lives, numbers such as 11:11, 12:34, 5:55, etc., show up for them. Often there is a question in their minds that they don't belong here on Earth. All believe there is life on other planets and that they have encountered a being of light. They have a sense of urgency to fulfill their mission and are sensitive to sound, light, odors, and colors. Usually, they are survivors of a life-threatening illness, severe accident, or trauma.

Crystal Children: Born 1995 and later. Crystal children are more involved than Indigos and look to the future of our Earth. They are the most peaceful, kind, and loving souls and are highly psychic. This being said, they are more abstract and extremely sensitive towards the environment. Born with magnetic personalities, there is no problem with discussing Angels, spirit guides, and past life memories, which makes it easy for them to be healers. They love crystals and rocks, integrity and truth. Because of their capacity for telepathic communication, they may be labeled "slow" or autistic. This is not the case.

Rainbow Children: Born 2000 and later. Being the third generation of special children, Rainbows are the children of pure love. Being the new ones on Earth with no incarnate, Karma, totally trusting and entirely fearless of everyone. Usually born to Crystal scouts that came in the 1980s. These children have never been to Earth before and are here to generate unconditional love with loads of empathy. They will play an important role of the future of evolution and humanity as they get older. Being totally trusting, they are all about service.

Diamond Children: Born 2010-2011. These are the children of purity, possess the most psychic capabilities, and realize that negativity is poison. Also first timers here on Earth. Diamonds depend on Earth's energy to shift to higher frequency in order to accommodate the influx of the critical mass of other Diamonds that will be coming in. Diamonds are fully embodied with Divine light. They are most comfortable with telepathic communication and can manifest almost instantly. They have no concept of anger, hate, fear, greed, or separation because they have never experienced the densities of Earth. They don't get into the drama that takes place on Earth and hold the DNA that allows those who are ready to overcome the illusion of this world. Many will be healers and can instantly awaken those that seek it.

Whatever may come, you now know why you feel different. These qualities have been seeded, fertilized, and are unique. It takes us years to finally become who we are. Once you are where you need to be, you will realize that it was all worth it.

Look for the qualities of each and see which one resonates with you. It has been said many times in this book: you are here for a reason. The goal is to find the reason and make it your mission to have the abundance that is yours. Each of you is different but the same.

You have the power within you to be all that you can be at any given moment. Just feel what is natural for you. Once you do this, it will all fall into place.

Above all, believe in yourself. You are the key to your own happiness. Once you are happy, you will see others that share this feeling.

Message from my Guys

We have kept our writings silent for a little while so that you can read, understand, and contemplate these pages. It is important for you to understand what has been written. There are so many different aids and ways that can help you along your journey. With the help of all that there is on our Earth you can become the full physical soul that you were meant to be. We ask that you don't just read these pages, but further your mind with all that you can to the full extent of what you are capable of in your here and now. This is a wonderful time for you with all the technology that is available.

Seek out any question, look for answers, dig down deep, and quench whatever thirst that you have. As long as you have the internet, your answers are there. As you are looking, we can point you in the right direction as long as you are aware that we are here. Pay attention to your inner feelings on what it is that you need answered.

Tinker has just touched the tip of the iceberg of knowledge that is available. Don't settle for one way or the other. Look for your truth and it will shine bright in your eyes when you see it. As it has been said: try, try again. Keep doing what you feel is necessary to become the spiritual being that you were meant to be. It is all there for you to discover.

Keep yourself to task and put in a little time each day to help yourself in your quest. All of you on Earth have the wisdom and capability to make the best out of everything.

It is up to you to push yourself and see the magnificent being that you are. We are here to help guide you along the way.

There are things that you will find when researching that you never thought about before, but once you see them, they will ring like a fine bell.

There will probably be a feeling of victory when something in particular comes to light. Get to truly know yourself inside and out. Be the warrior that you were meant to be!

Being in the non-physical, it is only our intention to help. We cannot do anything for you until you realize we are here and you give us permission to guide you in the direction that you need and want to go. If you tell us to go away, that is what we have to do. Nothing can be done until you are fully aware and ask for guidance.

Many seek guidance but after being helped turn it into more of the ego wanting to make its place known. Ego can hold back anything that is good and pure. With that you will find that some of the great happenings that you experienced have stopped coming through like before. Be aware of what is going on around you. Is it your heart and soul asking? Or has your ego entered where it doesn't belong?

Everything that you have strived for is here. Be pure in what you need and want. Remember Tinker's rule: Gratitude with Attitude. The more you give to others, the more you get in return. It does not have to be money. Kindness goes a lot farther! But we cannot help you when ego is involved. We have to wait until the realization hits you and you can see what is happening around you.

Keep trying, and never give up! We cannot say this

enough. Everything is a turn and twist; nothing is a straight road. Let your true self shine through. Help others as much as you can.

It is a great pleasure to us when your light shines brightest. This means that we have done right and have done our job well. With all this, the Divine feels this too! That wonderful, pure, magnificent vibration is going out from you and healing all around you—and us!

*Life is too short to wake up
in the morning with regrets.
So, love the people
who treat you right,
forgive the ones who don't,
and believe that everything
happens for a reason.
If you get the chance,
take it.
Nobody said it'd be easy,
they just promised it would be
worth it.*

Dr. Seuss

Conclusion

It is time for this book to come to an end. My Guys and I have tried to cover what it is to wake up and realize your potential and communicate with your Guys. The more you try to get in balance, the more you will see that there is so much out there for you. All of us, each and every person, want to be what we feel in our hearts and souls. So, I'm going to turn this over to my Guys and let them give you their final message.

A final message from my Guys

It has been a wonderful journey coming together with Tinker and going forth with this book. It has taken her many moments to realize what needed to be done. Once she dedicated herself to the task, it was easy from there.

We on the Other Side of the veil are waiting with great anticipation for you in the physical to come forth and be a shining light. It gives all of us great pleasure to be able to communicate with all of you.

We would like to explain a little further on how things work on this side. Maybe if you get a better understanding, it will open you up to new horizons.

One way to understand how we do what we do is to look at the life of a honey bee. These wonderful creatures come together as an organic community. Everything they do it is an "All for one" effort.

At times they go out from the hive and take part in their individual assignments, but they always come back to be with the others in their community. Once they are all together there is a beautiful flow and a type of dance and communication where they all know what is where at any given time.

For us in the non-physical, we are a very large community that work together as one. Our souls are all connected just like yours in the physical world, but we have no interference from other things that life on Earth has for you. Each of us is still an individual, but at the same time we are all together. We have our assignments, which are to guide you in the physical and help you be what you were destined to be. There is also a connection for you to have just as we do, and we try to get you to the place where you can connect with others and be that organic community.

This is where Tinker's writing comes in. She has been trying to answer questions in her mind of the what and where all her life. We have been with her guiding and pointing her in the right direction where she looked for answers. Everything she has put in this book can guide you to become a soul that can communicate with your non-physical beings and receive the guiding light you have been searching for.

We see so often that others take advantage and try to only turn a profit from those that seek an answer. We want you to be able to relate on your own. Therefore, we have guided Tinker to many different subjects throughout her life and now they are here for you to delve into. It is our hope that with this "how to" guide, you will be able to go forth and do what Tinker does with us, whether that be dreams, working with stones, or just realizing what kind of child you are there in the physical. Hopefully, upon reading this, things will start to connect for you, like completing a puzzle. Once all the pieces are together you will see the beautiful picture that has unfolded.

Once it's on its way to being achieved, it is our greatest hope that you will meet others that are doing the same, and all of us in the non-physical and physical can work together to make all life better. Better for you, better for your new friends, better for the creatures of Earth, and better for Earth herself. If this flow starts, you will see great things happen for you and everything around you. There will be great abundance in everything. It will be like a ripple when you throw a rock into water. The ripples grow larger and larger the farther out they go.

There will be times of turmoil. Not from what you do but from the resistance of those that refuse to see what is really out there for them. We see that at times it is hard to keep in the positive energy flow, and it can be an effort on your part to find your way back from where you were. Just remember that your Guys never leave you and are there to guide you to where you need to be.

We have found that on the physical plane you need to be able to go inside of your conscience and be aware of what it is actually there for you. Being able to relate to is the biggest and most powerful building block. You must realize that many of us have been in physical form and understand what it is to stay on your path.

For us in the non-physical that are with you, may have at times been together as a family or close friend when we were physical. As for myself speaking in the non-physical to Tinker, she and I have spent many moments together on Earth. Sometimes it is easier for us in the non-physical to relate to you if we are familiar with the soul that is occupying Earth in the physical plane. To be more specific, Tinker and myself were together as a united couple. The first time was when she was a Lemurian. This is how far back your spiritual family can go—and even farther. As you can see, this is where the life of the honey bee relates. We are all connected as an organic community.

There will be times when you will meet someone and the feeling of having already known this person will be overwhelming. The reason for this is: you *have* known them before. Somewhere, at some time, your paths have crossed, and it is time for them to cross again. Pay special attention to this when it happens. There is a reason for it.

Always—and we mean always—pay attention to any and all feelings you have. It is part of your soul to recognize different energy vibrations that are around you. Be attentive to that first impression or a feeling of potential regret. This is one of the ways that we can in the non-physical let you know that we are here for you. This is one of the ways that the communication between us is done. We will try every way possible to help you on your physical path.

We know that you have many questions on how this takes place, and we want to give you answers. Therefore, you in the physical world need to find any way possible to connect with us. It is better to get the information you need now and firsthand. Why wait for answers when they are at your beck and call?

Look at the moments in your life when you could start relating, the moments in your childhood when books were read to you or you decided to read them for yourself. So many were written for the purpose of being able to connect with the non-physical. Pinocchio had Jiminy Cricket, Dumbo had Timothy Q. Mouse, and it goes on and on. The authors of these wonderful books were in connection with those on the Other Side and they were guiding the authors with messages. We have always strived to find a way for that light inside of you to turn on. The more you strive to make it happen, the brighter your light will be.

Now let us try to explain the meaning of time in the non-physical. As you have been told earlier in this book, most of the references are done in moments. For us on the Other Side, it is a longer moment than what you in the physical can relate to.

We "see" moments because we realize that once we have crossed over, life is infinite and forever. We see a larger horizon of things that could happen. It is like being on a mountain top looking out over the vastness. There is the realization of what is coming, like the storm that is approaching or the movements of clouds to show the sun coming through. This is what we can relate to you to beware of or let you know that good things are coming.

We in the non-physical can predict things in the near future. But, we know that if enough of you come together to change them, these predictions *can* be changed for the good. You in the physical know of the environment and weather changes, the coming extinction of species and so on. Therefore, we emphasize the coming together for good, positive energy that is there for all. This one act of kindness—going forth in a positive way—will make a difference.

As we said earlier, this is a call to arms. There needs to be a positive connection between us here and you there. One worker honey bee cannot do much, but the whole hive can devastate what is happening. We want a revolution—a revolution of starting and winning for the good of all. To be able to see that a difference is being made.

To have you in the physical be happy and joyous makes a difference in how all things are perceived. You can become a seer like so many others. Work with all that want to make the difference. Let us all become honey bees. Just imagine how beautiful and wonderful it will be, and watch what unfolds. It is a very simple and easy task for all.

At this moment, a new year is beginning for you there on Earth. Many of you are starting new resolutions to become in some way a better person in your physical body. We watch with great anticipation that this is the moment that you will connect with us and make this a new beginning for yourself. We open our arms and want to take you into that positive energy and vibration that can guide you to being what you were meant to be.

We see so much potential in all of you. Many of you in the physical are downtrodden and are trying to pull yourselves out of the hectic life that pulls you down. Please see that there is always a brighter day, a happier time, and we are trying our best to lift you up. Call on us, just ask us to help. Keep hope in your heart. We are here!

When Tinker pulls back, she can always relate to something in nature. Through the years she has been collecting stones and crystals and has learned the meaning of each kind. At this moment, she has a beautiful stone of labradorite with her in her lap. The reason for this is the weather; she is battling a sinus condition. The stone helps her at this particular moment; it helps her go within and continue to make this book happen because it is as important to her as it is to us.

The point we are making is: there is always something on Earth that can help you awaken. As we have said, there are times that you will not be as bright of a light as other moments in time. Reach out and find what works for you. Study and look for what different knowledge is there to help you. When it appears to you, you will know. Your own vibrational energy will tell you: this is it! We will also help you by giving our signs of approval. Everything that is worth it will give you a wonderful feeling of glow and positive vibration. It may even be something from your past that brings back happy moments. Seek it out!

Even as this book comes to a close, we will continue to work with Tinker and have her keep a log of thoughts and happenings that may help in the future. As we go forward it is our hope that others will read the messages and contemplate making themselves into their full potential.

Remember that in the physical you have what other creatures don't, which is free will. It is all up to you.

*Be a light unto yourself.
Do not follow others, do not imitate,
because imitation, following, creates stupidity.
You are born with a tremendous
possibility of intelligence.
You are born with a light within you.
Listen to the still, small voice within,
and that will guide you.
Nobody else can guide you, nobody else can
become a model for your life,
because you are unique.
This is your glory, your grandeur—that
you are utterly irreplaceable, that you
are just yourself and nobody else.*

*Osho
The Dhammapada: The Way of the Buddha, vol. 2*

The Aftermath

The starting of a new chapter after the book has finished. My Guys felt it was necessary to do this. They made sure I got the book done by the beginning of March 2020, and I have since started to try to find someone that would be interested in publishing.

And then it happened. They had been trying to let me know it was coming. You see, we have a deal, my Guys and myself. I have always made it clear that if something is coming down the pike, I don't want to get messages of panic or dire straits from them. Everything is to be kept matter of fact; just let me know what I need to do to make sure that everything is taken care of. They have kept their side of the bargain to make sure that there is no need for me to worry or have to handle much strife or mental anguish.

They have been making sure that I hear what they say. Through the book they were letting us know that something was on its way to us and we needed to prepare. (If you let your Guys come through and listen to what they tell you, your butt is covered.)

I had them guide me to a job that I truly care about. I don't make a lot of money but I'm happy with what I do, and it has ended up being what is now known as an essential job. It is one of the financial needs that everyone relies on, and I am very thankful to my Guys that they found the position for me.

As they were letting me know to get prepared for the inevitable through many conversations of us going back and forth, one thing that I did ask for was to make sure whatever was that was coming that I would have all my bases covered as far as money goes and have everything fixed that needed to be fixed. There is a new roof on my house (if you remember from a previous chapter). Also, I have a new HVAC system, and the alternator and starter on my vehicle are new.

You are probably thinking, "How in the hell does she get messages from her Guys as to what to fix and when?" It's all about getting a sign. Pay attention to what is going on around you. This is also covered in the book, as you have already read. I've covered the roof and explained how that went down. My HVAC was sinking fast, and I knew that was a sign that it needed to be replaced. Through listening and following what was put in front of me, I happened upon a new unit at a really good price.

One of the kids in the neighborhood that my sons grew up with had been working in heat and air with his uncle all his life. He has since started his own business and when he got word through my middle son that I was having problems, he got in touch with me and promised that when a good deal came through, he would let me know. In the meantime, he did his best to keep the old unit going at about $20 a shot.

As for my vehicle: as you know, I grew up a tomboy and to fit in I had to have a little knowledge of various cars and trucks, including knowing how they worked. What my Guys did with that was to have something start to show signs of wear and tear. It's all about seeing the signs, paying attention, and then following through. A sluggish start when you turn the key is a sign that either the battery is going or the starter is about to give out. The battery had been replaced a while back and they are generally good for four to five years. So, that told me that the starter was on its last breath. Same with the alternator: when you step on the gas and the radio panel goes off and then when you let off the gas it comes back on, that's the alternator. My Guys always follow through. Once the signs are given, then the constant little nagging and prodding starts. They are in my ear! "You need to get that checked. When are you going to have that fixed?" At times it is like having an overly sweet but always in your face grandmother that means well.

Now down to business with what is happening in our world at this moment and how anyone that picks up this book can make a difference in how their life is going. So many of you are in a hardship that some don't understand. I was there at the beginning of 2009's Great Recession. It is not a very good place to be, physically or mentally. But you can make this better for yourself. As hard as it may seem, there is silver in the lining of those dark clouds. I'm about to turn this over to my Guys and let them help you help yourself. They are there waiting for you to ask for help. When you read their words, please listen to what they say.

Message from my Guys

We on the Other Side want to give you hope in this dark time. There are promises being made to you, and from looking from this side, those promises are not going to be upheld as hard as they try. It is time for you to depend on yourself and yourself only. It is time for you to get in touch with those that are there to pull you to safer ground. Please stop listening to those that have empty voices. Prepare yourself for what is going to be a long trip before you feel relief.

The first thing we suggest is to find a quiet essence

around you. Go within yourself and find what is waiting for you. Pull your thoughts away from strife, and go where those that truly care can be with you at this time. If possible, listen to the quietness that abounds around you. In that quietness are the voices that want to be heard.

Tinker finds her quietness listening to the birds sing. They are her alarm every morning. Their voices singing to the new day brings harmony to her life. She is happy to know that there are those creatures that, no matter what is going on with Earth and its inhabitants, sing their praise and gratitude for a new day.

Once you find yourself within, focus on what you need to do to make yourself and those around you better. Alienate what is happening with the present disaster that is being played out by those of ego and greed. Be aware that they do not have your best interests at heart. Pull away from listening to what is being said on TV and listen to what is said within. The answers are there. Focus on what your small voice inside is saying.

This is a time to find others that have the same outlook and band together, just as the singing birds do each day. Their individual songs together make a harmonious energy that can be felt by everyone. Yours can too. Look for those people that have become a part of thinking for themselves and wanting to be able to make it without being influenced by the thoughts of others. Your numbers are many, your single thoughts can join together, and you will find that your world and theirs will start to make a difference in what is happening.

Yes, there is a virus that is wreaking havoc on all, but have faith in yourself and your own intelligence to make it through this without having to rely on those that will take advantage and not be there when the time comes. Rely on those that can also see through what is happening and want to make this a new beginning for all. Those that do not have your best interest will become smaller and less significant if you and the ones that see life for what it is band together and let it be known that enough is enough.

We call upon you to make the difference that needs to be done. We see a turn that can be made for the better. There is hope, and we are here to guide you to a better place and environment.

First, ask for what you need to do next. The answer will come with the guidance of your Guys. Don't ignore any small thought or action that comes to you. You will feel gentle nudges, so please don't ignore or have second thoughts. It is time to act because you deserve better! You will be surprised by how frequently help is there.

It is up to you to listen and make the difference in your own life. You all are gifted and have the ability to be all that there is to offer. If the feeling of despair comes in, just ask for help! The answer is there, and you should take advantage of it.

Time for me to intervene:

I have learned through the years not to take anything for granted. I've gotten over the push to have lots of money or a bigger and better home. My goal is to be happy. Having possessions does not buy happiness. My life is simple, and I wouldn't have it any other way.

Because of this, I feel richer than I could ever be otherwise. I have good health and great sons. I love my dogs and have everything I need. It's because I listened and followed what was put in front of me. Every day I hear those around me wanting more and more of everything material. But for me as long as there is a roof over my head, food in my mouth, and laughter around me, I am rich! Richer than they will ever be. Happiness is the greatest medicine that has ever been invented.

My Guys have been patient with me and, yes, when I went through the stage of wanting all the shiny glorious trinkets and toys, they pulled back and just let me make my mistakes. Once they realized what was going on and how unhappy I had become, they were there for me. No blame or "I told you so," just there to help me be happy again. You can do this too; it just takes a small amount of time to get in tune and listen to what is really available.

Back to my Guys

It is important to let things go! Do *not* hold onto the thoughts that all is negative and there is no way for you to pull out of this. There is always a way! If you let your own Guys come to you and listen to that one little voice, the dark and gloomy will subside. Keep your faith that all will be well because you know you have help.

Remember, there is power in numbers. Keep your awareness open for others that are striving to do and make a better environment for all. Do not dwell on that what was but look forward to what is. You are mightier than you know!

As we close on this please remember to always be thankful and realize you are what you make yourself to be. Keep reaching out to your own Guys and be grateful that they are there to help. It is with all the love we give you that will make this possible.

We are sure that you and many others will benefit

from all we have put down in this book. There is hope, so do not ever forget that you can have a wonderful and eventful life.

About Atmosphere Press

Atmosphere Press is an independent, full-service publisher for excellent books in all genres and for all audiences. Learn more about what we do at atmospherepress.com.

We encourage you to check out some of Atmosphere's latest releases, which are available at Amazon.com and via order from your local bookstore:

Out and Back: Essays on a Family in Motion, by Elizabeth Templeman

Just Be Honest, by Cindy Yates

You Crazy Vegan: Coming Out as a Vegan Intuitive, by Jessica Ang

Detour: Lose Your Way, Find Your Path, by S. Mariah Rose

To B&B or Not to B&B: Deromanticizing the Dream, by Sue Marko

Convergence: The Interconnection of Extraordinary Experiences, by Barbara Mango and Lynn Miller

Sacred Fool, by Nathan Dean Talamantez

My Place in the Spiral, by Rebecca Beardsall

My Eight Dads, by Mark Kirby

Dinner's Ready! Recipes for Working Moms, by Rebecca Cailor

About the Author

In 1957 "Tinker" was born in Albuquerque, New Mexico. A natural bookworm and researcher, she extended her skills in business, and developed writing to word in layman's terms for everyone concerned to understand.

With the advice of her "Guys" she has put her writing skills and ways of expressing her thoughts with theirs onto paper helping all find the answers they seek through their own Spiritual Beings.

Self-proclaimed believer in energies and vibrations the Guys gave her the knowledge, that abundance is more than money. They live life to the fullest with many smiles and blessings.

CPSIA information can be obtained
at www.ICGtesting.com
Printed in the USA
LVHW090345270821
696168LV00004B/268